RAPE

RAPE

by

Irving J. Sloan

**Law for the Layperson
Oceana's Legal Almanacs, Second Series**

**Oceana Publications, Inc.
Dobbs Ferry, NY**

Rape. Sloan, Irving. 191 pages

ISBN: 0-379-111713
ISSN: 1059-5376

Copyright 1992 by Oceana Publications, Inc.

Printed in the United States on acid free paper.

TABLE OF CONTENTS

CHAPTER 1

THE FIRST ELEMENT OF RAPE:

Actual penetration is required as an element of rape, and penetration constitutes sexual intercourse, once more commonly termed "carnal knowledge." Although some states still use the common law expression, many jurisdictions are now using the term "sexual intercourse."

Although some penetration must be shown beyond a reasonable doubt in order to sustain a conviction, it need not be full penetration, and the slightest penetration is sufficient.

> "The essential guilt of rape consists in the outrage to the person and feelings of the victim of rape. Any sexual penetration, however slight, is sufficient to complete the crime." - *Cal. Penal Code, §263*

In an Arizona case, evidence was held sufficient to establish a slight penetration even though the defendant was impotent and had no erection at the time of the act. In another case in California the court said that penetration alone is sufficient, there need not be any bleeding.

Emission is not an essential element of the crime of rape, so that emission without penetration is not sufficient. It is not necessary that the hymen be ruptured although evidence that it was may prove penetration.

1

RAPE

In a number of states, sexual intercourse means, for the purpose of rape, not only intercourse in the ordinary sense but also intercourse with the mouth or anus.

"Sexual penetration means sexual intercourse, cunnilingus, fellatio, anilingus, or anal intercourse." - *Colo. Re. Stats. 318-3-401 (6).*

"Sexual intercourse means penetration of the vulva, anus or mouth of one person by the penis of another person, or penetration of the vulva or anus of one person by any body member of another person or penetration of the vulva or anus of one person by any foreign instrument or object manipulated by another person for the purpose of arousing or gratifying the sexual desire of either party." *ALI Model Penal Code, §213.1 (1)*

As the Penal Code provides, penetration may be committed by an object manipulated by the accused into the genital or anal opening of the victim's body. This means that in those jurisdictions, of which there are several following the Code, penetration need not be by the penis, but can be accomplished with a foreign object like a stick or a baseball bat. Thus, the Virginia statute provides that:

"A. An accused shall be guilty of inanimate object sexual penetration if he penetrates the labia majora or anus of a complaining witness who is not his spouse, other than for a bona fide medical purpose, or causes such complaining witness to so penetrate her own body with an object or causes a complaining witness, whether or not his spouse, to engage in such acts with any other person or to penetrate, or be penetrated by, an animal. . ." - *Code of Virginia, §18.2-67.2. (See Appendix A, for complete section, "Inanimate object sexual penetration")*

Maine also deals with object penetration:

"Any act involving direct physical contact between the genitals or anus of one and an instrument or device manipulated by another person when that act is done for the purpose of arousing or gratifying sexual desire or for the purpose of causing bodily injury or offensive physical contact." - *Maine Revised Stats. Ann §251, 1 (c) (3)*

Entry of the anterior of the female genital organ, known as the vulva or labia, is sufficient for forcible or statutory rape and it is not necessary that the vagina itself be penetrated or that the hymen be ruptured.

A number of jurisdictions have expressly or impliedly held that simply touching or a mere contact of the sexual organs is not sufficient to constitute the element of penetration necessary to sustain a conviction of rape or statutory rape.

Because it is not essential that penetration be proved by the testimony of the victim but may be established by circumstantial evidence, the presence or absence of evidence of particular physical facts has been found relevant in many of the cases that involve the question of the sufficiency of the evidence as to penetration.

In *Hice v. State,* 593 S.W.2d 169, the testimony of a nine-year-old victim, coupled with that of the examining physician who found irritation, redness, and tenderness within her labia but no injury to the hymen or evidence of penetration beyond, was held to be sufficient to establish the defendant's guilt under the rape statute prohibiting "penetration, however slight, of a vagina by a penis." A victim's testimony that "He tried to put his male sex organ into my female sex organ. He couldn't do that, because I'm a virgin and he couldn't get through. He kept trying everything, hugging and kissing me," proved penetration through inference that the defendant's male sex organ penetrated the victim's vulva or labia until restrained by her intact hymen. The California court, *People v. Karsai,* 182 Cal.Rptr. 406, stated that the penetration standard in the rape statute required neither vagina be entered nor hymen ruptured.

On the other hand, there are cases where these very same physical circumstantial evidentiary facts were held insufficient evidence of penetration. The courts would note that the injury, or the rupture of the hymen might have resulted from other causes, or that the complaining victim's blood-stained underclothing was shown not to have been on her at the time of the alleged attack, or that an emission by the defendant without penetration did not constitute the crime of rape. The Mississippi statute provides that when the accused is charged with sexual intercourse with a female under age 12, the prosecution need not show penetration but only that the private parts of the female have been lacerated or torn in an attempt to have sexual intercourse.

A final example of a finding of penetration by way of circumstantial evidence is where testimony by expert witnesses and forensic evidence that the victim suffered vaginal laceration at the vaginal entrance, that the dome of the vagina was reddened as if struck by something, that Type A blood consistent with the victim but inconsistent with the defendant was found on the bed, on defendant's clothes and in his pubic area, and that the blanket on the victim's bed contained residue of seminal fluid, although there was no evidence of ejaculation in the vagina, the Virginia court held it was sufficient to establish penetration even though the victim testified she was uncertain as to whether penetration had occurred. *Elam v. Commonwealth*, 229 Va. 113, 326 S.E.2d 685.

CHAPTER 2

WHO MAY COMMIT RAPE?

Rape, in its *general* definition, may be committed only by a male and it may be committed only upon a female. There are a variety of social purposes and a background of the laws that restricted rape as a crime which could be committed only by males against females. There is the goal of protecting females from sexual attacks and, perhaps, forced pregnancies. Statutes still in effect and language in the case law of many states indicate that some special sensitivity to females as females is involved: "the essential guilt of rape. . . consists in the outrage to the person and the feelings of the *female,*" reads the Oklahoma statute (emphasis added). This perception of the female as a unique creature, harmed in some unique way by untoward sexual behavior, for a long time precluded any thought that sex crimes should protect males as well. Such a proposition was dormant even after legislative changes in the common law of rape had expanded the crime to a point where the law proscribed behavior by males that could just as easily be achieved by females, for instance, the seduction of an incompetent.

Some thirty-eight states now have rape laws which apply their proscriptions equally to both sexes: Alaska, Arizona, Arkansas, Colorado, Connecticut, Florida, Hawaii, Iowa, Kansas, Kentucky, Maine, Maryland, Massachusetts, Michigan, Minnesota, Missouri, Montana, Nebraska, New Hampshire, New Jersey, New Mexico, North Carolina,

RAPE

North Dakota, Ohio, Oklahoma, Pennsylvania, Rhode Island, South Carolina, South Dakota, Tennessee, Texas, Utah, Vermont, Washington, West Virginia, Wisconsin, and Wyoming. *(See Appendix A for the statutory language.)*

In the remaining "minority" states rape is still a "one-way" or male-only crime. Thus the Alabama statute:

> (a) A male commits the crime of rape in the first degree if:
>
> (1) He engages in sexual intercourse with a female by compulsion; or (2) He engages in sexual intercourse with a female who is incapable of consent by reason of being physically incapacitated; or (3) He, being 16 years or older, engages in sexual intercourse with a female who is less that 12 years old.

Alabama Code §13A-6-61(a)

The other minority states that fail to apply their rape laws equally to both sexes are: California, Georgia, Idaho, Illinois, Mississippi, Nevada, New York, Oregon, and Virginia.

A number of these states do have laws relating to "deviant" sex crimes which apply equally to both sexes, but because the definition of "deviant" does not include normal vaginal intercourse, these states can still be fairly characterized as using gender classifications in their laws on sex offenses. Furthermore, penalties for rape are more severe than penalties for deviant intercourse in some of these minority states. Such states also tend to have statutory rape laws which punish males and protect females without extending their proscriptions to female seducers of young males. This means that in states where rape itself is still a male-only crime, unequal treatment of males and females is still a feature of the law, despite reforms in the deviant sex crimes laws.

By contrast, the majority of states now proscribe a wide variety of nonconsensual sexual impositions in statutes equally applicable to both sexes. Distinctions between normal intercourse and "deviant" sexual activity are typically abolished, the rationale being that all of these nonconsenual impositions are equally abhorrent. In some states the crime is still called "rape"; others label it "criminal sexual conduct" or "sexual assault". As described in the preceding chapter, the crime usually encompasses unlawful "sexual penetration", which is characteristically broadened far beyond normal intercourse and includes "cunnilingus, fellation, anal intercourse, or any intrusion, however slight, of a genital, or of any object into the mouth or anal openings of another person." The following states have this kind of wording in their statutes: Colorado, Connecticut, Florida, Michigan, Minnesota, Nebraska, New Hampshire, New Jersey, New Mexico, North Dakota, Ohio, South Carolina, South Dakota, Tennessee, Vermont, Washington, West Virginia, Wisconsin, and Wyoming. *(See Appendix A for the statutory language.)*

RAPE

Current state laws, then, cover a wide range, from the traditional law with its inherent gender distinctions to the most modern gender-neutral laws. The movement toward making sex offenses gender-neutral is probably an inevitable response to new constitutional requirements. The commentary in some of the statutory materials suggest this explanation.

Actually, however, decisions have gone both ways where the courts have passed upon the constitutionality of both forcible and statutory rape laws which limit the protection of females only or punish only males.

A few examples will indicate the differing reasoning and approaches. *Brinson v. State*, 278 So. 2d 317, held unconstitutional a Florida state statute which made it a crime to rape a female, but did not extend the same protection to males. Observing that males are entitled to the same protection from degrading ravishment and sexual assaults, regardless of the orifice involved, as are females, and that it is no longer consonant with constitutional principles for equal protection to continue a criminal sanction against sexual assaults on females and not provide the same criminal sanction where such assaults are made on males. The state statute that made such a limit to its protective provisions was violative of the state constitution and the Fourteenth Amendment of the United States Constitution.

WHO MAY COMMIT RAPE?

A Federal court affirmed a judgement granting habeas corpus relief to a prisoner convicted of statutory rape under a New Hampshire statute making it a felony for a male to have sexual intercourse with a consenting female, without making it a crime of any kind for a woman to have normal sexual intercourse with a male under the age of 15. The court held that the gender based classification was violative of the Fourteenth Amendment of the United States Constitution.

In *Tatro v. State*, 372 S. 283, the Mississippi Supreme Court, considering a statute which prohibited any male above the age of 18 from handling, touching, or rubbing with any part of the body any child under the age of 14 when done for the purpose of "gratification of lust, or of the indulging depraved licentious sexual desires," held the statute unconstitutional. The court said that since women were as capable of performing the prohibited physical acts as men, there was no rational basis for making the statute applicable only to men.

For all practical purposes, the law of sex crimes is undergoing a rapid change toward complete sex-neutrality. The prevailing sensitivity in the Supreme Court to claims of sex discrimination is making the earlier male only laws unable to survive equal protection of the laws of scrutiny.

A 1979 Supreme Court case, *Orr v. Orr*, 440 U.S. 268, established the trend invalidating male-only sex laws. In *Orr*, the Court found that an Alabama

statute which allowed alimony to women but not to
men violated the equal protection clause. Noting
that statutes which distribute benefits and burdens
on the basis of gender "carry the inherent risk of re-
inforcing stereotypes about the 'proper place' of
women and their need for special protection", the
Court stated that, "A gender-based classification
which, as compared to a gender-neutral one, gener-
ates additional benefits only for those it has no reason to prefer cannot survive equal protection
scrutiny." This 1980 High Court decision turned
the tide away from male only sex laws.

CHAPTER 3

CONSENT

The rape victim's lack of consent has always been an element of the crime of rape. The act of sexual intercourse must have been accomplished against the victim's will or without her consent. These terms are viewed as being synonymous and they are frequently used interchangeably. While some jurisdictions still use the expression "against her will," there is a strong tendency today to use the language "without her consent."

> "Lack of consent.- (1) Whether or not specifically stated, it is an element of every offense defined in this Chapter that the sexual act was committed without consent of the victim." *Kentucky Rev. Stats. Ann. §510.020.*

Conceptually, "lack of consent" results either from the defendant's use of force or threatened force, or from the victim's *incapacity* to consent.

Use Of Force Or Threat Of Force

Where the defendant uses force or threatens to use force, there is no consent. It is not the force which accompanies the act of penetration but the force used or threatened to overcome or prevent resistance by the victim. The most common term in the statutes to express this idea is "forcible compulsion."

> (a) A person commits rape if he engages in sexual intercourse or deviate sex sexual activity with another person:

RAPE

(1) By forcible compulsion; or. . .

Arkansas Code of 1987 §5-14-103.

Such forcible compulsion usually means physical force, or an express or implied threat of death or physical injury to any person as well as kidnapping of that person.

(2) 'Use of Force' means: (A) Use of a dangerous instrument; or (b) use of physical force of violence or superior physical strength against the victim.

-Connecticut General Stats. Ann. §53a-70b.

(g) The term 'serious personal injury' means great bodily harm or pain, permanent disability, or permanent disfigurement.

-Florida Stats. Ann. §794.011.

"The defendant compels the victim to submit by force or by threat of imminent death, serious physical injury, extreme pain, or kidnapping, to be inflicted upon anyone, or by any other threat which would compel a reasonable person under the circumstances to submit."

-Kentucky Rev. Stats. Ann. §510.010(2)

Resistance

One of the major problems in the discussion of rape is posed by the amount of resistance a woman must put up for the act to be defined as a rape rather than as a response to indications that she is:

14

CONSENT

(1) ambivalent about her intentions; (2) quite will-
ing if the male can be sufficiently persuasive; (3) or,
is pretending to resist when she is actually playing
a teasing game, wanting to be begged and finally
taken. Rape involves and implies resistance.

Most states have eliminated the earlier requirement of "utmost resistance" to establish nonconsent. The victim's state of mind at the time of the
assault was crucial to proving nonconsent. Since
one's state of mind is subjective, this element is difficult to prove. The extent of the force used by the
rapist and the amount of resistance on the part of
the victim became the means to help prove lack of
consent. However, even if a prosecutor could show
considerable force, the victim's state of mind had to
be introduced into evidence. The reliance on subjective lack of consent as an element in the crime leads
to serious policy questions. How much force must
there be to vitiate any apparent consent? To what
extent must a victim resist before lack of consent is
presumed?

There are, generally, three theoretical standards
for resistance. The first of these is that the victim
must do everything in her power to resist the attack. This is called the "utmost" or "uttermost"
standard which, as has been pointed out, no longer
prevails among any of the states. The second, the
"reasonable" resistance standard, demands that the
victim do only what is reasonable given the circumstances of the case. Finally, it is rape even if the victim does not resist if she can show that her

15

submission was the product of fear or grave bodily injury.

The courts shifted in the period from about 1910 to 1940 from the utmost standard to the reasonable standard. State statutory law began to reflect that change starting in the 1970s. This shift was essentially due to the fact that judges and legislators came to realize that the utmost standard could, when strictly applied, lose sight of the issue of consent and demand resistance for its own sake. The utmost standard could ignore real dangers to the woman in continuing to struggle. If necessary to avoid being murdered, most women would submit to being raped, yet the threat of murder may not involve any evident physical force. Furthermore, such standards cannot consider the circumstances of the crime. There is often a fine line between the resistance necessary to negate consent and actions which may increase the violence of the assailant. A woman may rightly fear that resistance in any form would result in serious physical injury or even death, and act accordingly.

> "(6) When the charge is forcible rape, the fact that the act of intercourse was performed forcibly and against the will of the complaining witness is a necessary element of the crime which must be proved beyond a reasonable doubt. The degree of force exerted by the defendant and the amount of resistance on the part of the complaining witness are matters that depend upon the facts of the particular case. Thus we have

CONSENT

held that resistance is not necessary under circumstances where resistance would be futile and would endanger the life of the female as where the assailant is armed with a deadly weapon, and that proof of physical force is unnecessary if the prosecuting witness was paralyzed by fear or overcome by superior strength of her attacker. It is, however, fundamental that in order to prove the charge of forcible rape there must be evidence to show that the act was committed by force and against the will of the female, and if she has use of her faculties and physical powers, the evidence must show such resistance as will demonstrate that the act was against her will."

-*People v. Fauslisi,* 25 Ill. 2d 457, 185 N.E.2d 211.

"In the case at bar, it does not appear that the defendant used the prosecutrix roughly at the onset or at any time; he made only the one threat- that he would kill her if she made outcry- before the intercourse, and that the threat was made while they were both in the buggy. He never told her how he was going to kill her; he never exhibited or intimated, that he had a gun or knife, or any sort of weapon. She says she was scared, but she does not say just how her fright affected her. She did not plead with the man to desist. She said nothing, except when her glasses fell off. the she said, 'Be careful'. On the witness stand she said she spoke that way about the glasses because she did not want to lose them, for she could not see without them."

-*State v. Morrison,* 189 Iowa 1027, 179 NW 321

A number of states include "resistance" or "earnest resistance" in their definitions of "forcible compulsion"

Rape is an act of sexual intercourse accomplished with a female under either of the following circumstances:

(3) Where she resists but her resistance is overcome by force or violence.

-*Idaho Code §18-6101*

In short, resistance is not required if resistance would be futile or foolhardy. The victim can decide not to resist when she is paralyzed by terror beyond the point of being capable of making a decision.

A number of the statutes focus on the actions of the rapist rather than the consent of the victim. For example, certain circumstances have been categorized as so dangerous by some jurisdictions tha the sexual act is defined as a crime regardless of the victim's state of mind. These include rape in conjunction with the following situations: use of a dangerous weapon, serious physical injury to the victim, during the commission of a felony such as a kidnapping or breaking and entering, involuntary administration of drugs or alcohol to the victim to the point she becomes incapacitated, where the vic-

CONSENT

tim is vulnerable due to youth or a special relationship to the rapist by blood or position of authority, and threats of serious injury or death to the victim or to a third person.

The California statute is perhaps the most comprehensive provision among the state statutes dealing with the incapacity of consent.

(1)Where a person is incapable, because of a mental disorder or developmental or physical disability, of giving legal consent, and this is known or reasonably should be known to the person committing the act.

(2)Where it is accomplished against a person's will by means of force, violence, or fear of immediate and unlawful bodily injury on the person or another.

(3)Where a person is prevented from resisting by any intoxicating or anesthetic substance, or by any controlled substance, administered by or with the privity of the accused.

(4)Where a person is at the time unconscious of the nature of the act, and this is known to the accused.

(5)Where a person submits under the belief that the person committing the act is the victim's spouse, and this belief is induced by any artifice, pretense, or concealment practiced by the accused, with intent to induce the belief.

(6)Where the act is accomplished against the victims will by threatening to retaliate in the future against the victim or any other person, and there is a reasonable possibility that the perpetrator will execute the threat. As used in this paragraph "threatening to retaliate" means to kidnap or falsely imprison, or to inflict extreme pain, serious bodily injury, or death.

(7)Where the act is accomplished against the victim's will by threatening to use the authority of a public official to incarcerate, arrest, or deport the victim or another, and the victim has a reasonable belief that the perpetrator is a public official. As used in this paragraph, "public official" means a person employed by a governmental agency who has the authority, as part of that position, to incarcerate, arrest, or deport another. The perpetrator does not actually have to be a public official.

-West's Ann. California Codes §261

The defendant in all of these situations must knowingly take advantage of the victim's incapacity to give consent to sexual intercourse.

In any prosecution under this chapter in which the victim's lack of consent is based solely on her incapacity to consent because she was. . . mentally defective, mentally incapacitated or physically helpless, the defendant may prove in exculpation that at the time she engaged in the conduct constituting the offense she did not know of the facts or conditions responsible for such incapacity to consent.

-Kentucky Rev. Stats. Ann. §510.030

Fraudulently Obtained Consent

Consent obtained by fraud may or may not be vitiated. Many cases considering the question whether sexual intercourse accomplished under the pretext of medical treatment is rape. Cases involving rape by a physician by means of administration of drugs so as to overcome the will of the woman to resist are not included in this discussion because this kind of situation is dealt with in the previous section on the topic of "resistance."

The courts consistently hold that a conviction for rape is proper in cases where a physician, while purporting to treat a female patient, had sexual intercourse with her, either against her protest or by surprising her. In *State v. Atkins,* 292 SW 422, where a physician had sexual intercourse with a female patient while he was supposedly making a vagina examination, and the patient, because of embarrassment, had her eyes closed and covered with one arm, it was held that the physician could be convicted of rape under a statute providing for such conviction of one "forcibly ravishing any woman of the age of 16 years or upward."

"If it is rape under our statutes for a man to have illicit sexual intercourse with a woman while she is asleep, and incapable of consenting, when no more force is used than is

21

necessary to effect penetration with the consent of the woman, we are unable to see why it is not also rape for a man to have improper sexual intercourse with a woman by accomplishing penetration through surprise, when she is awake, but utterly unaware of his intention in that regard. In such case the woman is incapable of consenting, because she has no opportunity to give consent any more than has a sleeping woman. It would indeed be a reproach upon our statute if a physician, under the pretense that it was necessary for a woman patient to submit to examination of her sexual organs in order to assist him in the diagnosis of her ailment, and under the pretense that it was necessary for her to expose her person and assume a position which, at the same time, incidentally, afforded ready opportunity for sexual attack, could safely take advantage of her position and make an unexpected and uninvited sexual invasion of her person. If, under such circumstances, a physician takes such an unconscionable advantage of the woman's position, and, to her complete surprise, and, without the slightest ground to assume that he has her consent, violates the trust and confidence imposed in him and perverts her position and his opportunity into an unwanted and cowardly attempt to gratify his lust, the force merely incident to penetration should be deemed sufficient force within the meaning of our rape statute."

CONSENT

While the words and phrases in this 1926 Missouri opinion come across as quaint today, the reasoning and legal conclusions remain current. However, it should be noted that if the woman consents to sexual intercourse after having been persuaded to believe that medical treatment in the form of sexual intercourse was necessary, the defendant is not guilty of rape on the theory that even though the consent was induced by fraud it was with respect to a collateral matter.

If sexual intercourse follows a feigned marriage and the defendant was aware of the sham, but the woman was unaware, it is held that there is no rape. Generally, the courts hold that rape is not committed where the facts showed an impersonation by the defendant of a woman's husband in order to procure the intercourse. However, many jurisdictions have statutes that make the husband-impersonator deemed guilty of rape.

> Any person who falsely impersonates the husband of any married woman, and thereby deceives, and by means of such deception, gains access to her, and has carnal knowledge of her, shall, on conviction, be punished at the discretion of the jury, by death, or by imprisonment in the penitentiary for not less than ten years; but no conviction must be had under this section on the unsupported evidence of the woman.
>
> *Arizona Rev. Stats. Ann. §13-140 (5) (d)*

RAPE

Contributory Negligence

Proof of *negligence* is not, an absolute defense to rape (marital exemption). In theory, the courts defend the right of the foolish or even the "teasing" woman to make the final decision about sexual intercourse.

In *Keeton v. State*, 190 S.W. 2d 820, the defendant met the complainant for the first time at the cabin where the alleged rape subsequently occurred while she was there as the date of another man. On the night of the alleged rape, she voluntarily accompanied the defendant to this same cabin in company with another couple, who then left it. Apart form going to the cabin voluntarily, there is no evidence that she had any intention of consenting to sexual relations with the defendant. However, had she such intentions, the court here defends, in principle, her right to change her mind and to have her final refusal accepted.

> "Even if she had gone to the cabin on this occasion with appellant with the express purpose and intention of engaging with him in sexual relationship, and even though she had remained for that purpose after the other couple had left the cabin, still she had a right to change her mind and to refuse to carry out such intention or any other promise relative thereto."

This is a statement of the anti-coercion principle. It also represents the protection of the right of a

CONSENT

woman who might be toying with the idea of illicit intercourse to draw back.

While contributory negligence does not diminish the woman's right to say "no," it is sometimes taken as evidence that she did not exercise it.

It appears, then, that contributory negligence by the victim in a rape case occupies a status similar to prior chastity. The negligent woman, like the previously unchaste one, has the right to refuse sexual intercourse. She is in theory the victim of a rape if she is then forced against her will and without her consent. Again, however, contributory negligence can mitigate punishment. Finally, it seems to produce a diminishment of sympathy for the victim which can color the perceptions of other evidence or otherwise effect indirectly the outcome of the case.

Notice: Immediate Complaint

Resistance, previous sexual conduct, and contributory negligence are all variables considered by the courts in determining whether or not a woman was raped. The final variable considered by the court is the issue of immediate complaint or immediate outcry, sometimes termed "notice." Did the victim report a rape to some third party at the earliest possible moment after the assault? Or did she wait for some period of time before complaining of the attack?

"The federal principle of law is that whether or not the complaining victim "made prompt complaint of the alleged outrage to those to whom she would naturally complain" has "bearing on the question of consent.". Evidence of immediate complaint is not admitted "as proof that the crime was in fact committed, or as evidence of the truth of the facts complained of." It is admitted "to rebut the inference of consent that might be drawn form her silence" and to meet "any possible inference of self-contradiction in her conduct in the absence of a complaint." "Rape," **Corpus Juris Secundum**, Vol. 75, pp. 523-4

In short, the immediate outcry rule is that failure to make known the offense at the earliest possible opportunity creates a presumption against rape.

Court opinions have held that it helps to prove a rape when the woman overcomes her shame of admitting participation in a "sordid event" and reports the crime immediately. Courts have reasoned that her complaint doesn't help her cause, but that a failure to report it would have hurt her. Other courts have held that failure to report the crime was clearly due to shame and has no probative value on the question of rape. Yet some courts have concluded that a victim's failure to report is clear evidence of sham, despite obvious and oft cited explanations for such a failure in women who were really raped.

In Utah, no prosecution may be instituted unless the alleged sexual offense was brought to the notice of public authority

(a) Within three months of its occurrence or

(b) Where the alleged victim was less than eighteen years of age or otherwise incompetent to make compliant, within three months after a parent guardian, or other competent person specifically interested in the victim, other than the alleged offender, learned of the offense.

-Utah Code Ann. §76-5-407(2) See also Model Penal Code §213.6(5), Appendix A

A large number of states have statutory provisions similar to the Utah statute.

Connecticut, in order "to guard against stale claims in situations where blackmail is a possibility and where evidence may be difficult to obtain after a passage of time," no prosecution may be instituted unless the alleged sexual offense

. . . was brought to the notice of public authority within one year of its occurrence, or, where the alleged victim was less than sixteen years old or incompetent to make complaint, within one year after a parent, guardian or other alleged victim learns of the offense.

RAPE

-Conn. Gen. Stats. Ann. §53a-69

What should be noted in these states is that case law and in a few jurisdictions while still requiring making complaint from a few months to as long as a year, the prompt or "immediate outcry" rule does not apply

Rape Trauma Syndrome (RTS)

The rape trauma syndrome (RTS) is one kind of post-traumatic stress disorder. The essential feature of post-traumatic stress disorder is the development of characteristic symptoms after a psychologically traumatic incident that is usually beyond the range of ordinary human experience. Those symptoms typically involve experiencing the traumatic incident; numbing of responsiveness to, or lessened involvement with, the external world; and a variety of autonomic, dysphoric, or cognitive symptoms. The traumatic event can be re-experienced in various ways. Often the person has recurrent painful memories of the incident, or recurrent dreams or nightmares in which the incident is reexperienced. Diminished responsiveness to the external world, called "psychic numbing" or "emotional anesthesia," usually starts soon after the traumatic incident. A person may complain of feeling detached or estranged from others, that she or he has lost the ability to become interested in activities that were previously meaningful and enjoyable, or that the ability to feel emotions of any type- and particularly those associated with intimacy, tenderness, and sexuality- is significantly lessened. After the incident, many people develop symptoms of excessive autonomic arousal, including hyperalertness, and insomnia. Other symptoms characteristically arise, as well.

Although RTS first was developed to aid in the *treatment* of rape victims, it is now being used in rape prosecutions. In recent years, courts have been asked to decide whether RTS evidence is admissible in criminal cases. When consent is an issue in a rape trial many state courts have allowed RTS evidence to prove lack of consent. The courts in Arizona, Colorado, Kansas, Maryland, Montana, New York and Oregon have admitted testimony RTS evidence to corroborate testimony of the victim, but not to establish that a crime had been committed or have admitted such testimony when consent was an issue. On the other hand, other courts such as the supreme courts of California, Minnesota, and Missouri have held that expert testimony on RTS is inadmissible to prove that a rape occurred on various grounds ranging from that RTS was not developed to make that kind of determination to the conclusion that testimony on RTS generally is not recognized in the scientific community.

The Model Penal Code bars prosecution unless the complainant notified the public authorities within three months of the event. At the time the Model Code was drafted, failure to make a prompt complaint did not bar prosecution for a sex offense in any jurisdiction, but evidence of prompt notification to the authorities was admissible to rebut a suggestion of fabrication by the complainant. A few states did have special statutes of limitation for rape. At the present time, the Model Code has been followed in a large number of jurisdiction either by adoption or their won modification of the Model Code provision.

Although RTS first was developed to aid in the treatment of rape victims, it is now being used in rape prosecutions. The courts have reached different results on the admissibility of expert testimony on the rape trauma syndrome, or on the emotional or psychological stress symptoms typically exhibited by rape victims.

Under particular circumstances, the courts have on occasion held that such testimony was not admissible on the ground of irrelevance, its prejudice outweighing its probative effect, lack of reliability or scientific acceptability, absence of the expert's qualifications, invasion of the jury's province or rendition of an opinion on the ultimate issue.

Corroboration

The corroboration requirement for charges of rape did not exist at common law. The common law made one exception to the doctrine that the evidence of one witness may sustain a conviction of a crime: the rule that the testimony of one witness, without corroborating circumstances, is insufficient to sustain a conviction of perjury. In prosecutions

CONSENT

for rape or any other sexual offense, the common
law did not require corroboration.

A number of jurisdictions have historically required corroboration of the testimony of the alleged
female victim in prosecutions for sexual offenses.
The reasoning behind this was that it minimizes
the risk of false charges and that it balances the
sympathy for the victim felt by the jury. Beyond
this, it is argued that such a requirement is appropriate in view of the difficulty of defending against
a charge of rape, an offense that usually has no witnesses and takes place in a secluded setting. Not
only do some states, wither by statute or by judicial
decision, require that the testimony of the victim
must be corroborated in order to sustain a conviction for rape, a few states additionally require corroboration in certain circumstances such as for
statutory rape of an under-age female, or for forcible rape of an older woman where the case is otherwise weak, or for prosecutions arising from belated
complaint. Massachusetts and New Mexico demand limited corroboration in the sense of facts
and circumstances consistent with the complainant's testimony.

New York law removed the need for corroboration
of identity, except for statutory offenses, and leaves
its requirement of corroboration of force. Corroboration of penetration is not required but in its place is
added a requirement of some "other evidence tending to . . . establish that an attempt was made to en-

gage the alleged victim in sexual intercourse. . . at
the time of the alleged occurrence."

There is no requirement in any jurisdiction that
there be direct eyewitness testimony as corroboration of any part or element of the offense. Among
the facts which can be used as corroboration of force
are: physical signs of recent violent intercourse, the
condition of clothing, hysteria of the complainant,
and prompt complaint to legal authorities.

Finally, some states that do not impose any form
of corroboration requirement require a cautionary
instruction along the lines suggested by the Model
Penal Code requiring a cautionary instruction to
the jury.

> . . . to evaluate the testimony of a victim or
> complaining witness with special care in
> view of the emotional involvement of the
> witness and the difficulty of determining the
> truth with respect to alleged sexual activi-
> ties carried out in private.

CHAPTER 4

THE MARITAL EXEMPTION

Until recently, the courts were nearly unanimous in holding that a husband could not be convicted of rape, or assault with intent to commit a rape, upon his wife as the result of a direct sexual act committed by him upon her person. Rape laws developed at a time when a woman was considered the property of either her father or her husband. Thus rape began as a crime against property, not the person. The victim was not the woman assaulted, but instead was her husband. In this view, a husband forcing sex on his wife was merely making use of his own property.

What has come to be known as the marital rape exemption today, originated as common law with a statement made in the 17th century by Lord Matthew Hale who declared, "but the husband cannot be guilty of a rape committed by himself upon his lawful wife, for their mutual matrimonial consent and contract the wife hath given up herself in this kind unto her husband, which she cannot retract." Hale's rationale was that when a woman marries, she gives up her rights to her body because she has formed a contract with her husband which cannot be retracted.

A related rationale underlying the husband's immunity derives from the common law unity of person principle: upon marriage the legal identity of a wife merged into that of her husband. As another legal scholar in the 18th century, Blackstone, described it, "the very being or legal existence of the woman is suspended during the marriage, or at least is incorporated and consolidated into that of the husband under whose wing, protection, and cover she performs everything." This concept of women in marriage made rape by a husband impossible since a man cannot rape himself.

For over 300 years Hale's statement alone served as a justification for a spousal immunity involving rape charges, and was the origin for judicial recognition of the marital rape exemption in the United States. It also served to maintain the position of men in our society as dominators and women as their property.

The first American case in which the husband and wife were married and living together at the time the rape occurred was *Frazier v. State* 48 Tex. Crim. 142, 86 S.W. 54 (1905) in which the wife attempted to get a divorce from her husband but was refused by the court. Therefore, she stayed in the same house with her husband, but slept in a separate bedroom. When the husband forced himself upon her, the wife brought charges. The court adopted the common law, stating, "all the authorities" hold that a man cannot rape his wife. The husband's conviction was reversed.

These legal fictions, labeling a woman as her husband's property or "his other half" should have been discarded by the end of the 19th century with the

THE MARITAL EXEMPTION

adoption of the Married Women's Property Acts in almost every state. Those acts allowed a wife to hold and convey property, make contracts, and sue and be sued as if she were unmarried. Even in the area of personal torts, in which the majority of courts still refuse to recognize a law suit between spouses, an increasing number of jurisdictions have abolished interspousal exemptions and allowed a wife to sue her husband for negligence, assault, and other personal torts. The courts rejected the reasoning that personal tort actions between husband and wife would disrupt and destroy the peace and harmony of the home. Furthermore, the criminal law concept that the husband and wife are one and therefore cannot conspire with one another, has disappeared.

In most areas of the law, then, interspousal immunities and wives' disabilities were removed along with the legal fictions on which they relied. It is not surprising that, as we shall see, the current trend in both the legislatures and in the courts is to constrain and even abolish the prevailing marital rape exemption.

The rape trial of John Rideout in 1978 was perhaps the first case to make public the issue of marital rape. Prior to this case, no husband living with his wife at the time of the alleged offense had been prosecuted. The case was brought under Oregon's revised statute, which abolished the exemption preventing prosecution of the husband for raping his wife. Although John Rideout was acquitted, the issue had been raised and the public was made aware that husbands do not have unrestricted access to their wive's bodies.

The cases in which a wife-rape victim has successfully pressed charges against her husband generally arise in the context where the couple is separated at the time of the offense.

One case which did not arise in a situation where the couple was separated at the time of the alleged rape was *State v. Rider*, 449 So. 2d 903, a 1984 Florida case. In this case, Mr. and Mrs. Rider were living together as man and wife, no dissolution of marriage action had been instituted, and no temporary restraining order or judicial decree of separation had been obtained at the time of the rape. Furthermore, it was apparent that this was the first time Mr. Rider had sexually abused his wife. Although this factual pattern was contrary to the general trend established in previous cases, the court refused to recognize a common law "interspousal exception" to prosecution under Florida's sexual battery statute.

The more recent cases that have confronted the issue of marital rape appear to be favoring the wife-victim, particularly where the parties were separated at the time of the alleged offense. The *Rider* case suggests that the courts are beginning to respond favorably to the wife who is raped by her husband even though they were living together as man and wife.

THE MARITAL EXEMPTION

Perhaps the most far reaching judicial decision concerning the marital rape exemption was handed down in 1984 by the New York State of Appeals in *People v. Liberta*, 474 N.E. 2d 567. The defendant-husband, while living apart from his wife pursuant to a family court order, forcibly raped and sodomized his wife in front of their two and one-half year old son. Although the New York statute contained an express marital exemption, the defendant was prosecuted under an exception to the marital exemption that made it inapplicable to spouses living apart pursuant to separation agreements or certain court orders. The defendant-husband appealed the application of the exception and, in case he was treated just as any other unmarried male, he challenged the constitutionality of the rape and sodomy statutes as violative of the equal protection of the state and federal constitutions. He alleged that the statute burdened some but not all males, *i.e.* all but those within the marital exemption. The court agreed that the statute was unconstitutional, not because, as Liberta contended, it burdened some men and not others, but because distinguishing between marital and nonmarital rape caused the statute to be underinclusive.

Specifically, while the equal protection clause of the Fourteenth Amendment does not prohibit a statute from making classifications, the law cannot arbitrarily burden a particular group of individuals. If marital status is to be a classification, it must be reasonable and must be based upon "some ground of difference that rationally explains the different treatment." The *Liberta* court found no rational basis for distinguishing between marital and nonmarital rape. The court's conclusion was based on an analysis and rejection of the historical justifications to spousal immunity.

The *Liberta* court found Lord Hale's rule of supposed consent "untenable": "Rape is not simply a sexual act to which one party does not consent. Rather, it is a degrading, violent act which violates the bodily integrity of the victim and frequently causes severe, long-lasting physical and psychic harm." The court viewed the contention that consent would ever be given to such an act as absurd and noted that marriage is not a license to rape with impunity because a woman's right to control her own body is the same both in and out of wedlock. Marriage is no longer properly viewed "as giving a husband the right to coerced intercourse on demand." The court flatly rejected the other traditional justifications of women as property and the unity of person principle as being long outdated.

The *Liberta* decision is consistent with courts in other jurisdictions then and since which have found after analysis of the marital exemption that there is no modern justification for it. The rationale for this is that sexual assault is a violation of person's body and mind, and should be punished accordingly without regard to the relationship between the victim and the perpetrator of the crime.

THE MARITAL EXEMPTION

The present trend of rape laws do not exempt spouses from its prohibitions or the specific statutes do so under more limited circumstances than in the past. However, not all states have revised their laws in this respect, and among those states that have, the immunity accorded spouses varies greatly. At least none of the states provide in their statutes that marriage to the victim is a complete defense to a charge of rape, with no exceptions for *de jure* or *de facto* separations.

At the other extreme providing that marriage is never a defense, New Jersey, Oregon, and Delaware have eliminated the marital exemption *en_toto*.

> "No actor shall be resumed to be incapable of committing a crime under this Chapter because of age or impotency or *marriage*"
>
> -*New Jersey Stat. Ann. §2C:14-(b)*

In between is a bewildering variety of laws. Under some, only *legal* marriage is a defense, not cohabitation: Maine, Maryland, Michigan, Missouri, New Hampshire, New Mexico, New York, North Dakota, South Carolina, Washington, and Wyoming are such examples of this.

> 'Spouse' means a person legally married to the actor but does not include a legally married person living apart from the actor under a de facto separation.

> "Rape- with any person, not his spouse, and the person submits as a result of compulsion."

RAPE

-Maine   Rev.   Stat.   Ann.   17-A
§§251.1.A,252.1B.2

In other jurisdictions, including Alabama, Connecticut, Kentucky, Minnesota, Montana, Pennsylvania, and West Virginia, cohabitation as husband and wife is a defense.

> "In any prosecution for an offense under this part. . . it shall be an affirmative defense that the defendant and the alleged victim were, at the time of the alleged defense, living together by mutual consent in a relationship of cohabitation, regardless of the legal relationship of their relationship."

-Connecticut Gen. Stat. §53a-67(b)

Some states revoke the marital exemption if the spouses are only living apart: Alaska, Maine, and Pennsylvania.

> 'Spouse' means a person who is legally married and cohabitating."

-Arizona Rev. Stat. Ann. §13-1401

But Idaho requires 180 days of such living apart if no proceedings for divorce or separation have been filed.

> No person shall be convicted of rape for any act or acts with that person's spouse, except as provided hereafter:
>
> 1. A spouse has initiated legal proceedings for divorce or legal separation; or

THE MARITAL EXEMPTION

2. The spouse have voluntarily been living apart for 180 days or more.

-Idaho Code §18-6107

Colorado, on the other hand, requires that the de facto separation be with intent to love apart, although it is unclear just whose "intent" is required.

MARITAL DEFENSE. Any marital relationship, whether established statutorily, putatively, or by common law, between an actor and a victim shall not be a defense under this part 4 unless such defense is specifically set forth in the applicable statutory section by having the elements of the offense specifically exclude a spouse.

-Colorado Rev. Stat. §18-3-409

Several states revoke the immunity if spouses are living apart *and* one spouse has filed for separation or divorce: Indiana, Michigan, Minnesota, and Tennessee.

This section does not apply to sexual intercourse between spouses, unless a petition for

(1) Dissolution of their marriage;

(2) A petition for their legal separation, or

(3) A protective order under IC3 4-5-1; is pending and the spouses are living apart.

A person may not be prosecuted under this Article if the victim is the person's legal spouse at the time of commission of the alleged rape or sexual offense unless the parties are living separate and apart pursuant to a written agreement or a judicial decree.

-North Carolina Gen. Stat. § 14-27. 8

But the more popular view is to retain the defense until the separation or divorce decree has actually been granted: Examples of such provisions appear in the statutes of Kentucky, Louisiana, Maryland, Missouri, Montana, North Carolina (allowing, alternatively, a written separation agreement), North Dakota, South Carolina, Utah, and Wyoming.

Finally, it should be noted that the Model Penal Code *(See Appendix C)* preserves the traditional exclusion accorded husbands in that it defines, in part, the act of "rape" as sexual intercourse between a male and "female not his wife" and "sexual assault" as sexual contact between a person and another "not his wife." The Code's rationale is suggested in its Commissioner's Comment dealing with the Section 213 rape definition.

> . . . there is the case of intercourse coerced by or threat of physical harm. Here the law already authorizes a penalty for assault. If the actor causes bodily injury, the punishment is quite severe. The issue is whether the still more dramatic sanctions of rape should apply. The answer depends on whether the injury caused by forcible intercourse by a husband is equivalent to that inflicted by someone else. The gravity of the

crime of forcible rape derives not merely from its violent character but also from its achievement of a particularly degrading kind of unwanted intimacy. Where the attacker stands in an ongoing relation of sexual intimacy, that evil, as distinct from the force used to compel submission. may well be thought qualitatively different.

The notion that a wife who has been sexually imposed upon by her husband endures a less humiliating and degrading experience than an unmarried woman feels after being raped by a stranger, is a notion patently rejected by most legal writers today as well as by reform rape statutes. In fact it can be persuasively argued that the emotional and psychological impact of an unwanted sexual assault by a husband upon his wife are even more devastating. And this injury to an unmarried or married woman is the same and so it is foolish to talk about a "qualitative difference" warranting special consideration for a rapist husband.

There is today a recognition of the essential equivalence of all forms of nonconsensual sexual behavior in terms of the physical and psychological dangers involved. The law is shifting from prohibiting one sex from one particular form of sexual violation to a general condemnation of all forms of sexual violation, no matter who perpetrates it. Beyond this, protection is also being extended to those within the marriage relationship. Our statutory survey in this chapter indicates that this is what

RAPE

has happened in the topic of who can commit rape
in the law.

CHAPTER 5

THE RAPE VICTIM SHIELD LAW

Prior Sexual History

At common law, the rules governing the use of a rape complainant's sexual history provided that such evidence was always admissible. This probably goes back to the historical point made earlier in this volume that the early laws about rape and rape evidence reflected a moral climate in which women were expected to be chaste until married.

The laws developed not as much from a chivalrous need to protect women, however, as from a male need to protect his property. A woman was damaged if not a virgin, hence the severe penalties for a man who caused such damage. This historical notion explains the dichotomy between the high value placed on virginity and the extreme difficulty a woman faced in proving a rape charge.

Three elements combined to create the rule of admissibility of a rape complainant's sexual history. The first was the fear of false charges brought by vindictive women. Turning again to Sir Matthew Hale, Lord Chief Justice of the King's Bench in 16th century England, it was stated that rape

> "is an accusation easily to be made. . . and harder to be defended by the party accused, tho never so innocent."

RAPE

Second was the concept that chastity was a character trait. If a woman could be shown to be unchaste by nature, then it could be inferred that she had consented to sex with the defendant. Third was the belief that premarital sex was immoral. Acts of previous illicit sexual relations, like other acts of moral turpitude, could thereupon be used to impeach the credibility of the complaining victim in a rape case.

Typically, rape victim "shield" laws, as they are known, declare a general rule that evidence of a rape victim's prior sexual activities is "shielded" and therefore inadmissible. Furthermore, such a shield law statute creates a presumption that the defendant should not be allowed to introduce testimony on this point. We are also talking about the complainant's reputation for unchastity as well as her prior specific sexual acts. The reasoning behind this is one of irrelevancy. Modern works of psychology and sociology about current sexual mores appear to support the claim that consensual sexual intercourse on some occasions with some men, does not mean a woman necessarily consents to intercourse with anyone on any occasion. The argument is that in a sexually active society, there is no such thing as a "reputation for chastity." Defense lawyers in turn would argue that in trying to introduce extrinsic evidence of the complainant's prior sexual relations or her reputation for chastity, exclusion of such evidence or restrictions on cross-examination is an impermissible infringement of the defendant's right of confrontation.

THE RAPE VICTIM SHIELD LAW

Thus, outlawing all questions about a rape victim's past sexual history has been held to violate the Sixth Amendment which gives defendants the right to cross-examine and confront witnesses against them. Although defendants do not have the right to introduce evidence that is irrelevant or unnecessarily harmful to other people, they always have the right to introduce evidence crucial to their defense.

Two instances of special admissibility appear most commonly in state statutes (1) prior sexual relations with the defendant offered to show consent; and (2) a specific sexual act with another man to provide an alternative explanation for the physical indications of rape. The rape evidence laws universally allow the defendant who claims consent as a defense to show that he and the complainant had a prior consensual sexual relationship. Thus Missouri requires that the conduct be reasonably contemporaneous. Some states such as Massachusetts and New York permit only testimony concerning specific instances of conduct. Only evidence of prior sexual relations with the defendant is usually admitted.

Most jurisdictions provide that evidence of the complainant's specific sexual acts with persons other than the defendant's prior to the alleged rape is inadmissible on the issue of *consent* in a *statutory rape* prosecution because the complainant is deemed incapable is a rebuttable presumption or where, under the applicable statute, previous promiscuous intercourse on the part of the complainant is made a defense to the charge, exceptions to the general admissibility are supported.

The sexual behavior of the complainant may be admissible if it indicates an unusual pattern of consensual sexual activity that is closely related to the defendant's version of the events leading to his claim of consent. Florida, Minnesota and North Carolina so hold.

As a general matter, evidence of the complainant's sexual acts with persons other than the accused is inadmissible to impeach the complainant's *credibility* in a *statutory* rape prosecution. There are, however, cases which have recognized exceptions to this general rule of inadmissibility on the issue of credibility when the evidence tended to show that the complainant was a prostitute or that she may have fabricated the charges.

Almost all jurisdictions also permit the defendant to rebut evidence offered by the prosecution to corroborate the sex act itself-- presence of semen, resulting pregnancy or venereal disease, or the force inflicted-- by showing that such evidence may have been the result of a sexual act with another man at about the same time. A few jurisdictions allow such testimony to impeach the victim's credibility: California and Mississippi are examples of this. Two states, Maryland and Alabama, allow testimony of this kind to show a motive for fabrication. Vermont and Wisconsin allow evidence that the victim has previously filed false rape charges.

However, evidence is most often admitted dealing with the complainant's prior specific sexual acts *with the defendant* on the issue of the complainant's prior chastity, or as indicative of the amount of corroborating evidence necessary to support the complainant's testimony, or in mitigation of the defendant's punishment in the event of conviction.

A complainant's *reputation* for unchastity is usually admitted in a statutory rape prosecution on the issue of her prior chastity or lewdness, or in mitigation of the defendant's punishment in the event of a conviction, or, if the statute st provides, to reduce the charges against the defendant. For example, under a Kentucky statute providing that the punishment for one accused of raping a female child between the ages of 16-18 shall be 2-10 years unless the complainant is shown beyond a resonable doubt to be sexually immoral or to have such a reputation, the court held that evidence of her reputation for unchastity should be admitted even when there is a conflict as to whether she had reached the age of 16 at the time of the alleged offense.

Some states, however, provide by statute that evidence of the complainant's reputation for unchastity is not admissible in a *statutory* rape prosecution on the issue of whether she consented to sexual intercourse with the defendant, or on the issue of the complainant's credibility.

RAPE

A New Hampshire case, *State v. Howard,* 426 A.
2d 457, is a curious yet compelling example of a factual setting which will lead a court to admit evidence of even a young child's prior sexual history in
a statutory rape trial. The headnote speaks for itself:

> "Evidence that 12 year-old prosecutrix had,
> *inter alia,* masturbated bull, undressed
> young boys, had sex with father and grand-
> father, lived with man in apartment, and en-
> gaged in sexual activity with others while
> being shown on closed circuit television
> should have been considered as to admissi-
> bility upon pretrial motion, even under stat-
> ute proscribing evidence of prior sexual
> activity by statutory rape victim, evidence
> might have been admissible to show that
> prosecutrix had had sexual experience which
> could allow her to fabricate charge against
> defendant, to show that prosecutrix' life was
> such that there could be no doubt as to value
> she placed on telling truth, and to question
> why prosecutrix with vast experience would
> complain about sexual encounter with defen-
> dant."

What the holding in this case more than suggests
is that when the cir-
cumstances of the alleged victim's are overwhelm-
ing as they were in this case, the courts will skirt
around the statute that prohibits evidence of prior
sexual experience.

CHAPTER 6

STATUTORY RAPE

The rape laws in this country are all codified or covered by statute. Nevertheless, one comes across the terms "rape" and "statutory rape" so that there must surely be a distinction, and there is.

Since the time of Elizabeth I, rape statutes have distinguished between the forcible rape of adult woman and prohibited sexual relations with female children under a specific age. When states enacted criminal codes to codify the common law in the eighteenth and nineteenth centuries, formulations of the offense of rape characteristically followed the English law and distinguished between the rape of adult women and sexual relations between adult men and female children below a specified age. The Model Penal Code specifies 10 as the statutory age.

As the common law defense of consent developed in American law, the statutory age came to be designated the "age of consent" because proof of force or the absence of consent was not an element of the crime if the female was below the age specified by statute. This may be the appropriate time to note that the basic distinction between "rape" and "statutory rape" is in connection with the element of "consent." In a statutory rape prosecution the victim cannot be legally viewed as having given consent. Whether the victim is underage or is for one reason or another unaware of what is happening to her an a rape situation (she might be asleep, drugged, or duped by an impersonator of her husband of her husband), there can be no consent challenge by the defendant.

The terminology of consent became confusing, however, when many states enacted two distinct forms of statutory rape: the traditional formulation prohibiting carnal abuse of children under the age of 10 or 12, and a totally different formulation which prohibited "consenting" sexual intercourse with any female either under the age of 16 or 18 or between the ages of 12 and 16. These statutes were essentially equivalent to the English common law of seduction. This is what is usually referred to as "statutory rape."

The term "age of consent" therefore refers to the fact that consent of the victim is no defense in statutory rape. Twenty-one states retain a statutory provision which speaks of an age of consent: (Alabama (16), Alaska (16), Arizona (15), California (18), Delaware (16), Georgia (14), Idaho (18), Illinois (16), Kentucky (16), Massachusetts (16), Mississippi (12), Montana (16), New York (17), North Carolina (12), Oregon (18), Rhode Island (16), Utah (14), Virginia (13), West Virginia (16), and Wisconsin (15).

Most states have provided for a two- or three-tiered age system structure. States providing two statutory age classifications are Alabama, Connecticut, Indiana, Maryland, Michigan, Mississippi, New Hampshire, New Mexico, North Carolina, North Dakota, Tennessee, Wisconsin, and Wyoming. The following states have three basic age gradations: Kentucky, New Jersey, New York, Oregon, South Carolina, and Washington. Arkansas has more than three such classifications.

> A person commits carnal abuse in the first degree, a class C felony (forcible rape, "by forcible compulsion" or when the victim is "physically helpless" is a class A felony), when, being 18 years of age or older, he engages in sexual intercourse with a person not his spouse who is under 14 years of age; a person commits carnal abuse in the third degree, a class A misdemeanor, when being 20 years of age or older, he engages in sexual intercourse with a person not his spouse who is under 16 years of age; and a person commits sexual misconduct, a class B misdemeanor when he engages in sexual intercourse with a person not his wife who is under 16 years of age.

Ark. Stats. Ann., §§41-804, 806, 807

Until at least 1964 it was the almost universal rule that the defendant's knowledge of the age of the victim was not an essential element of the crime of statutory rape, and therefore it was no defense that the accused reasonably believed her to be of the age of consent. This disallowance of mistake as to age appears to spring from the common law definition of rape as including consensual intercourse with a female less than 10 years of age., as noted earlier here.

RAPE

In the past, the courts which have applied this rule justified or explained the divergence from the general requirement of guilty intent in a number of ways. One was the doctrine of transferred intent. This exception has also been justified on grounds of social policy. The interest of society in protecting children form the machinations of seducers and rapists outweighs whatever injustice may have been involved in doing away with proof of specific intent. While this argument may have been more persuasive in earlier times when the age of consent was comparatively low, it loses its force in those many jurisdictions today where the age of consent has been raised substantially.

Those who advocated statutory changes against the rule that knowledge of the child's age is irrelevant noted that no serious social policy of protecting the sexually immature and inexperienced female is likely to be involved in any situation where the defendant can make out a reasonable case for his belief that the victim was above the age of consent, and that to apply the rule strictly might lead to convictions of persons who are themselves the victims of imposture by fully experienced and aware, though young persons who under our social and sexual mores are permitted and encouraged to go into the world as women and even marry. Actually, even before the present trend of statutory change or reform, most of the cases which did in fact sustain a conviction for statutory rape as against a serious claim that the defendant acted under a reasonable mistake about the person's age have involved very young persons.

But as most states have extended the age of consent to 16, 17, or 18, they have at the same time adopted a compromise between the traditional rule of disallowing altogether mistake in the law of statutory rape and a general policy against strict liability.

Some examples of a few state statutes will illustrate this trend toward change. In Arizona it is a defense to a prosecution for "sexual conduct with a minor," where the victim's lack of consent is based on incapacity to consent because the victim was 15, 16, or 17 years of age, that "defendant did not know and could not reasonably have known the age of the victim." Arkansas provides that it is no defense where the victim is under age 11 that the defendant did not know the age of the child reasonably believed the child to be 11 years of age or older. But when the criminality of the conduct depends on a child being under a critical age which is older than 11, it is a defense that the defendant reasonably believed that child to be of critical age or older. On the other hand, Colorado still holds that it is no defense that the defendant did not know the child's age or even that he reasonably believed the child to be 15 years of age or older. Delaware also provides that it is no defense "that the actor did not know the child's age, or reasonably believed the child to be older than 16.

RAPE

Section 213.6(1) of the Model Penal Code provides that it is no defense to liability for rape or deviate sexual intercourse that the accused reasonably believed the child to be older than 10 years of age. Strict liability is thought to be acceptable for offenses based on such extreme youth. But Section 213.6(1) provides that the accused may defend in cases where the age is set higher than 10 by proving that he "reasonably believed" his sexual partner to be above the specified age. The defendant must establish the fact and reasonableness of his mistake by a preponderance of the evidence.

More than half the states have enacted revised statutes giving the defendant a defense if he affirmatively proves reasonable belief than his partner was older that the upper limitation of statutory rape. The result is that today a majority of jurisdictions if one includes those states that have adopted the Model Code position by judicial decision, have abandoned the traditional rule of strict liability for the upper age limit making the partner liable for consensual intercourse. Nevertheless, there remain a few states that do follow the traditional view and disallow the mistake defense completely, even for the higher ages made relevant to the various sexual offenses. Again, as has been pointed out throughout

STATUTORY RAPE

harsher penalties for sexual penetration offenses with very young children while narrowing the concept of what will be prohibited under the offenses which define consenting conduct among older teenagers. The principal age break seems to be at 12 or 16, with only a few states retaining a statutory age of 18 for prohibited consenting sexual conduct.

Because the age of consent is the crucial factor, not the willingness of the younger partner, the previous chastity is not held to be relevant although many courts take it into account as a mitigating factor in determining the punishment to be imposed on the male. This is in contrast to the law in forcible rape cases where the woman's previous promiscuity cannot be used as a defense by the accused if it can be shown that he used force, violence, or threat in inducing her to have sex, the defendant can invoke her promiscuity to establish the fact that he would not need to use force and in fact did not do so. The young or minor female, whom the law is designed to guide to protect, is likewise entitled to that protection no matter how unchaste she may have been. But the defendant cannot invoke her sexual history as a defense because the only points at issue are her age and whether the sexual intercourse took place.

CHAPTER 7

THE AIDS ISSUE IN RAPE

At this point of time in contemporary society, every rape victim is at risk to become infected with acquired immune deficiency syndrome, AIDS. The incubation period for the AIDS virus ranges from six to twelve weeks so that the only way a victim can immediately determine if she or he has been exposed to AIDS is to know whether the attacker is an AIDS carrier.

In 1988, California enacted an AIDS testing statute as part of the Penal Code. The legislature's express purpose in passing this statute was ". . . to benefit the victim of a crime by informing the victim whether the defendant is infected with the AIDS virus. It was also the intent of the Legislature. . . to protect the health of both victims of crime and those accused of committing a crime." The statute requires the court of issue a search warrant to obtain and test the accused's blood whenever the court has probable cause to believe that blood or semen was transferred from the accused to the victim. If the test result is positive, the results are confirmed and the disclosed to the victim. Note the statute specifically limits the test to informational purposes by providing that the results of the blood test may not be used in the criminal proceeding, nor as the impetus for a charging decision by the prosecutor. Since the results may not be introduced at trial, the defendant's right to a fair trial is protected.

The New York legislature also passed a comprehensive AIDS law that same year in 1988, as part of its Public Health Law. The New York statute differs from the California Statute in that it strictly limits mandatory HIV testing and it guarantees the confidentiality of test results.

New York limits testing by requiring that the test subject give written, informed consent to be tested unless he has put his HIV status in issue, or the test is authorized by law. In addition, the statute does not require informed consent if the individual is not competent to give his or her informed consent. In such case, the victim must obtain the consent "of a person authorized pursuant to law to consent to health care for the individual."

Neither of these exceptions gives the victim of a sexual assault the right to have the defendant tested for AIDS. The statute's first exception refers directly to a rule of the New York Civil Practice Laws and rules which is designed to aid discovery in civil trials where one of the parties, as part of a claim or defense, has placed his or her own physical condition in issue. This discovery rule does not apply to mandatory testing of person accused of sexual offenses because the victim's desire to test the defendant for HIV arises in a criminal context, and because the defendant has not put his own HIV status in issue second exception to the requirement of informed consent allows an HIV test to be performed if it is authorized or required by state or federal law. At the present time no state or federal statute mandates HIV of those accused of sex crimes. The only law that might be read to require such a test governs court ordered discovery. However, since there is no reason a prosecutor needs to discover the offender's HIV in order to prosecute, the victim should be unable to obtain a court order for a mandatory test.

The New York statute also guarantees the confidentiality of HIV test results. By ensuring such strict confidentiality of all HIV test results, the legislature indicated that it hoped to encourage voluntary HIV testing so that individuals would subsequently change their behavior to reduce the risk of transmission.

In certain limited applications, New York law allows health care providers, public health officers, adoption agencies, parole officers, and correctional facilities severely restricted access to HIV test results. The only time when the court may breach this confidentiality is upon an application showing "a clear and imminent danger to an individual whose life or health may unknowingly be at risk as a result of contact with the individual to whom the information pertains." In assessing clear and imminent danger, the statute instructs the court to "weigh the need for disclosure against the privacy interest of the protected individual and the public interest which may be disserved by disclosure which deters future testing or treatment or which may lead to discrimination."

EMERGING TRENDS IN RAPE LAW

Delaware, Illinois, Iowa, and Vermont also do not allow a sexual assault victim access to the defendant's test results unless the victim is able to demonstrate compelling need. In assessing compelling need, each of these state's statutes instructs the court to '(6weigh the need for disclosure against the privacy interest of the test subject and the public interest which may be disserved by disclosure which deters further testing or which may lead to discrimination."

There is as of now very little case law and not a great deal of statutory law among the state jurisdictions, but the reader should be aware nevertheless that a body of such case and statutory law is developing.

CHAPTER 8

DATE RAPE

Date rape is nonaggravated sexual assault, non-consensual sex that does not involve physical injury, or the explicit threat of physical injury. But because it does not involve physical injury, and because physical injury is often the only criterion that is accepted as evidence that the *actus reas* (the wrongful deed) is nonconsensual, what is really sexual assault is frequently mistaken for seduction. The replacement of the early rape laws with the new laws on sexual assault have done nothing to resolve this problem.

Rape, defined as nonconsensual sex, usually involving penetration by a man of a woman who is not his wife, has been replaced in some criminal codes with the charge of sexual assault. This has the advantage both of extending the range of possible victims of sexual assault, the manner in which people can be assaulted, and replacing a crime which is exclusive of consent, with one for which consent is a defense. But while the consent of a woman is now consistent with the conviction of her assailant in cases of aggravated assault, nonaggravated assault is still distinguished from normal sex solely by the fact that it is not consented to. Thus the question of whether someone has consented to a sexual encounter is still important, and the criteria for consent continues to be the central concern of discourse on sexual assault.

However, if a man is to be convicted it is not sufficient to establish that the *actus reas*, i.e., he must either have believed that his victim did not consent or that who was probably not consenting. In many common law jurisdictions a man who sincerely believes that a woman consented to a sexual encounter is deemed to lack the required *mens rea* (guilty knowledge and purpose), even though in fact the woman did not consent, and even though his belief is not reasonable.

The criteria for *mens rea*. for the reasonableness of belief, and for consent are closely related, for although a man's sincere belief in the consent of his victim may be sufficient to defeat *mens rea*, the court is less likely to believe his belief is sincere if his belief is unreasonable. If his belief is reasonable, they are more likely to believe in the sincerity of his belief. If his belief is reasonable, they are more likely to believe in the sincerity of his belief. But evidence of the reasonableness of his belief is also evidence that consent really did take place. For the very things that make it reasonable for *him* to believe that the defendant consented are often the very things that incline the courts to believe that she consented.

A woman on a casual date with a virtual stranger has small chance of bringing a complaint of sexual assault before the courts. One reason for this is the prevailing criterion for consent. According to this criterion, consent is implied unless some emphatic episodic sign of resistance occurred, and its occur-

rence can be established. But if no episodic act occurred, or if it did occur, and the defendant claims
that it didn't, or if the defendant threatened the
plaintiff but won't admit it in court, it is almost impossible to find any evidence that would support the
plaintiff's work against the defendant. This problem
is exacerbated by suspicion on the part of the courts
and police that even where an act of resistance occurs, this act should not be interpreted as a with-
holding of consent, and this suspicion is especially
upheld where the accused is a man who is known to
the female plaintiff.

One legal textbook of criminal law warns that
where a man is unknown to a woman, she does not
consent if she expresses her rejection in the form of
an episodic and vigorous act at the "vital moment".
But if the man is known to the woman she must, according to this legal writer, make use of "all means
available to her to repel the man." He goes on to
warn that women often welcome a "mastery ad-
vance" and present a token resistance. This suggested difficulty of distinguishing real protest from
pretense continues to be a major hurdle for women
who brings charges of rape or sexual assault.

The claim that the victim provoked a sexual incident, that "she asked for it," is the most common defense given by men who are accused of sexual
assault. A common "she asked for it" rationale is
the injunction against sexually provocative behavior of the part of women. If a woman should not be
sexually provocative, the, from this standpoint, a
woman who is sexually provocative deserves to suf-

fer the consequences. Of course women get raped
even when they are not sexually provocative and
men get to interpret what counts as sexually provocative. Thus do women to court heavily burdened
in the attempt to prove their charges. Given the
changes that have taken place in the rights of
women to be themselves and express themselves to
the same extent as men, why shouldn't a woman be
sexually provocative? Why should this behavior jus-
tify any kind of aggressive response whatsoever?

As a judge on the Supreme Court of New Hampshire, Justice David Saluter, now on the U.S. Supreme since 1990, rendered an opinion in a
"nonstranger" rape case which is fairly typical of
the rationale leading to acquitting defendants in
these kinds of cases.

In *State v. Colbath*, 130 N.H. 316, 540 A. 2d
1212(1988), Justice Saluter viewed the victim's conduct with other men that same afternoon as highly
relevant in determining whether the victim later
consented to sexual intercourse with the defendant.
More than this, he inferred consent from the fact
that the defendant and the victim had become ac-
quainted earlier in the day and had been seen
touching each other sexually. Other courts share
such assumptions about the relevance of the victim's prior acquaintance between victims and alleged rapists allows defendants more easily to
argue consent or, in the alternative, to argue that
they had a reasonable, good faith belief that the victim consented to sexual intercourse. Thus does the
prevailing law allow defendants to use a preexisting

DATE RAPE

relationship to give credibility to a defense of consent or reasonable, good faith belief of consent.

As matters now stand, victims in date rape or nonstranger rape stand small chance of turning their charges into convictions. The result is that most such episodes go unreported and rapists go home free.

APPENDIX A
SELECTED STATE STATUTES

SELECTED MISCELLANEOUS STATE RAPE STATUTES

ALABAMA

□ Ala. Code

Article 4
Sexual Offenses
§13A-6-60. Definitions

The following definitions apply in this article:

(1) SEXUAL INTERCOURSE - Such term has its ordinary meaning and occurs upon any penetration, however slight; emission is not required.

(2) DEVIATE SEXUAL INTERCOURSE - Any act of sexual gratification between persons not married to each other involving the sex organs of one person and the mouth or anus of another.

(3) SEXUAL CONTACT - Any touching of the sexual or other intimate parts of a person not married to the actor, done for the purpose of gratifying the sexual desire of either party.

(4) FEMALE - Any female person.

(5) MENTALLY DEFECTIVE - Such term means that a person is rendered temporarily incapable of appraising or controlling his conduct owing to the influence of a narcotic or intoxicating substance administered to him without his consent, or to any other incapacitating act committed upon him without his consent.

RAPE

(7) PHYSICALLY HELPLESS - Such term means that a person is unconscious or for any other reason is physically unable to communicate unwillingness to an act.

(8) FORCIBLE COMPULSION - Physical force that overcomes earnest resistance or a threat, express or implied, that places a person in fear of immediate death or serious physical injury to himself or another person.

§13A-6-61. Rape in the first degree.

(a) A male commits the crime of rape in the first degree if:

(1) He engages in sexual intercourse with a female by forcible compulsion; or

(2) He engages in sexual intercourse with a female who is incapable of consent by reason of being physically helpless or mentally incapacitated; or

(3) He, being 16 years or older, engages in sexual intercourse with a female who is less that 12 years old

(b) Rape in the first degree is a Class A felony.

§13A-6-62. Rape in the second degree.

(a) A male commits the crime of rape in the second degree if:

(1) Being 16 years old or older, he engages in sexual intercourse with a female less than 16 years old and more than 12 year old;

provided, however, the actor is at least two years older that the female.

(2) He engages in sexual intercourse with a female who is incapable of consent by reason of being mentally defective.

(b) Rape in the second degree is a Class B felony. (Acts 1977, No. 607, p. 812.)

ALASKA
Alaska Stat.

§ 11.41.410. Sexual assault in the first degree. (a) A person commits the crime of sexual assault in the first degree if,

(1) being any age, the defendant engages in sexual penetration with another person without consent of that person;

(2) being any age, the defendant attempts to engage in sexual penetration with another person without consent of that person and causes serious physical injury to that person;

(3) being over the age of 18, the defendant engages in sexual penetration with another person

(A) who the defendant knows is mentally incapable; and

(B) who is entrusted to the defendant's care

(i) by authority of law; or

(ii) in a facility or program that is required by law to be licensed by the Department of Health and Social Services.

(b) Sexual assault in the first degree is an unclassified felony and is punishable as provided in AS §12.55.

Sec. 11.41.445. General provisions. (a) In a prosecution under AS §§11.41.434 - 11.41.440 it is an affirmative defense that, at the time of the alleged offense, the victim was the legal spouse of the defendant unless the offense was committed without the consent of the victim.

(b) In a prosecution under AS §§11.41.410 - 11.41.440, whenever a provision of law defining an offense depends upon a victim's being under a certain, it is an affirmative defense that, at the time of the alleged offense, the defendant reasonably believed the victim to be that age or older, unless the victim was under 13 years of age at the time of the alleged offense.

MISCELLANEOUS STATE STATUTES

ARIZONA

□ Ariz. Stat. Ann.

Criminal Code
Title 13

§13-1401. Definitions

In this chapter, unless the context otherwise requires:

1. "Oral sexual contact" means oral contact with the penis, vulva or anus.

2. "Sexual contact" means any direct or indirect fondling or manipulating of any part of the genitals, anus or female breast.

3. "Sexual intercourse" means penetration of the penis into the vulva or anus by any part of the body or by any object or manual masturbatory contact with the penis or vulva.

4. "Spouse" means a person who is legally married and cohabitating.

5. "Without consent" includes any of the following:

(a) The victim is coerced by the immediate use or threatened use of force against a person or property.

(b) The victim is incapable of consent by reason of mental disorder, drugs, alcohol, sleep or any other similar impairment of cognition and such condition is know or should have reasonably been known to the defendant.

(c) The victim is intentionally deceived as to the nature of the act.

(d) The victim is intentionally deceived to erroneously believe that the person is the victim's spouse.

§13-1404. Sexual abuse; classifications

A. A person commits sexual abuse by intentionally or knowingly engaging in sexual contact with any person fifteen or more years of age without consent of that person or without consent of that person or with any person who is under fifteen years of age if the sexual contact involves only the breast.

B. Sexual abuse is a class 5 felony unless the victim is under fifteen years of age in which case sexual abuse is a class 3 felony punishable pursuant to §13-604.01.

§13-1406. Sexual assault; classification; increased punishment

A. A person commits sexual assault by intentionally or knowingly engaging in sexual intercourse or oral sexual contact with any person without consent of such person.

B. Sexual assault is a class 2 felony, and the person convicted is not eligible for suspension or commutation of sentence, probation, pardon, parole, work furlough or release from confinement on any other basis except as specifically authorized by §31-233, subsection A or B until the sentence imposed by the court has been served. If the victim is under fifteen years of age, sexual assault is punishable pursuant to §13-604.01.

C. Notwithstanding the provisions of §13-604 and §13-604.01, if the sexual assault involved the use or exhibition of a deadly weapon or dangerous instrument or involved the intentional or knowing infliction of serious physical injury and the person has previously been convicted of sexual assault, or any offense committed outside this state which if committed in this state would constitute sexual assault, the person shall be sentenced to life imprisonment and is not eligible for suspension or commutation of sentence, probation, pardon, parole, work furlough or release from confinement on any other basis except as specifically authorized by §31-233, subsection A or B until at least twenty-five years have been served.

§13-1406.01. Sexual assault of a spouse; definition; violation; classification

A. A person commits sexual assault of a spouse by intentionally or knowingly engaging in sexual intercourse or oral sexual contact with a spouse without consent of the spouse by the immediate or threatened use of force against the spouse or another.

B. A first offense sexual assault of a spouse is a class 6 felony. Pursuant to §13-702, the judge has discretion to enter judgment for conviction of a class 1 misdemeanor with mandatory counseling. Any subsequent sexual assault of a spouse is a class 2 felony and the person convicted is not eligible for suspension or commutation of sentence, probation, pardon, parole, work furlough or release from confinement on any other basis except as specifically authorized by §310233, subsection A or B until the sentence imposed by the court has been served. Convictions for two or more offenses not committed on the same occasion but consolidated for trial purposes shall not be counted as prior convictions for purposes of this section.

C. A person convicted under this section may, in the discretion of the court, be exempt from the registration requirements of chapter 38, article 3, of this title.

§13-1407. Defenses

A. It is a defense to a prosecution pursuant to §13-1404 and §13-1405, involving a minor, if the act was done in furtherance of lawful medical practice.

B. It is a defense to a prosecution pursuant to §13-1404 and §13-1405, in which the victim's lack of consent is based on incapacity to consent because the victim was fifteen, sixteen or seventeen years of age, if at the time the defendant engaged in the conduct constituting the offense the defendant did not know and could not reasonably have known the age of the victim.

C. It is a defense to a prosecution pursuant to §13-1402, §13-1404, §13-1405 or §13-1406, if the act was done by a duly licensed physician or registered nurse or a person acting under his or her direction, or any other person who renders emergency care at the scene of an emergency occurrence, reasonably believed that no one competent to consent could be consulted and that a reasonable person, wishing to safeguard the welfare of the patient, would consent.

D. It is a defense to a prosecution pursuant to §§13-1404, 13-1405 or 13-1406 that the person was the spouse of the other person at the time of commission of the act. It is not a defense to a prosecution pursuant to §13-1406.01 that the defendant was the spouse of the victim at the time of commission of the act.

E. It is a defense to prosecution pursuant to §13-1410 that the defendant was not motivated by a sexual interest. It is defense to prosecution pursuant to §13-1404 involving a victim under fifteen years of age that the defendant was not motivated by a sexual interest.

Arkansas

□ Ark. Stat. Ann.

§5-14-101. Definitions.

As used in this chapter, unless the context otherwise requires:

(1) "Deviate sexual activity" means any act of sexual gratification involving:

   (A) The penetration, however slight, of the anus or mouth of one person by the penis of another person; or

(B) The penetration, however slight, of the vagina or anus of one person by any body member or foreign instrument manipulated by another person;

(2) "Forcible compulsion" means physical force or a threat, express or implied, of death or physical injury to or kidnapping of any person;

(3) "Mentally defective" means that a person suffers from a mental disease or defect which renders him incapable of appreciating the nature of his conduct;

(4) "Mentally incapacitated" means that a person is temporarily incapable of appreciating or controlling his conduct as a result of the influence of a controlled or intoxicating substance administered to him without his consent;

(5) "Physically helpless" means that a person is unconscious or is physically unable to communicate lack of consent;

(6) "Public place" means a publicly or privately owned place to which the public or substantial numbers of people have access;

(7) "Public view" means observable or likely to be observed by a person in a public place;

(8) "Sexual contact" means any act of sexual gratification involving the touching, directly or through clothing, of the sex organs, or buttocks, or anus of a person or the breast of a female;

(9) "Sexual intercourse" means penetration, however slight of a vagina by a penis;

(10) "Guardian" means a parent, stepparent, legal guardian, legal custodian, foster parent, or anyone who, by virtue of a living arrangement, is placed in an apparent position of power or authority over a minor.

§5-14-102. In general.

(a) The definition of an offense excluding conduct with a spouse shall not be construed to preclude accomplice liability of a spouse.

(b) When the criminality of conduct depends on a child being below the age of fourteen (14) years, it is no defense that the actor did not know the age of the child, or reasonably believed the child to be fourteen (14) years of age or older.

(c) When criminality of conduct depends on a child being below a critical age older than fourteen (14) years, it is an affirmative defense that the actor reasonably believed the child to be of the critical age or above. The actor may be guilty, however, of the lesser offense defined by the age that he reasonably believed the child to be.

(d) When the criminality of conduct depends on a victim being incapable of consent because he is mentally defective or mentally incapacitated, it is an affirmative defense that the actor reasonably believed that the victim was capable of consent.

RAPE

§5-14-103. Rape.

(a) A person commits rape if he engages in sexual intercourse or deviate sexual activity with another person:

(1) By forcible compulsion; or

(2) Who is incapable of consent because he is physically helpless or

(3) Who is less than fourteen (14) years of age. It is an affirmative defense to prosecution under this subdivision that the actor was not more than two (2) years older than the victim.

§5-14-104. Carnal abuse in the first degree.

(a) A person commits carnal abuse in the first degree if, being eighteen (18) years old or older, he engages in sexual intercourse or deviate sexual activity with another person not his spouse who is less than fourteen (14) years old.

(b) Carnal abuse in the first degree is a Class B felony.

§5-14-105. Carnal abuse in the second degree.

(a) A person commits carnal abuse in the second degree if he engages in sexual intercourse or deviate sexual activity with another person not his spouse who is incapable of consent because he is mentally defective or mentally incapacitated.

(b) Carnal abuse in the second degree is a Class D felony.

MISCELLANEOUS STATE STATUTES

§16-42-101. Admissibility of evidence of victim's prior sexual conduct.

(a) As used in this section, unless the context otherwise requires, "sexual conduct" means deviate sexual activity, sexual contact, or sexual intercourse, as those terms are defined by section 5-14-101.

(b) In any criminal prosecution under §§ 5-14-103--5-14-110, or for criminal attempt to commit, criminal solicitation to commit, or criminal conspiracy to commit an offense defined in any of those §§, opinion evidence, reputation evidence, or evidence of specific instances of the victim's prior sexual conduct with the defendant or any other person is not admissible by the defendant, either through direct examination of any defense witness or through cross-examination of the victim or other prosecution witness, to attack the credibility of the victim, to prove consent or any other defense, or for any other purpose.

(c) Notwithstanding the prohibition contained in subsection (b) of this section, evidence directly pertaining to the act upon which the prosecution is based or evidence of the victim's prior sexual conduct with the defendant or any other person may be admitted at the trial if the relevancy of the evidence is determined in the following manner:

(1) A written motion shall be filed by the defendant with the court at any time prior to the time the defense rests stating that the defendant has an offer of relevant evidence of the victim's prior sexual conduct and the

purpose for which the evidence is believed relevant.

(2)(A) A hearing on the motion shall be held in camera no later than three (3) days before the trial is scheduled to begin, or at such later time as the court may for good cause permit.

(B) A written record shall be made of the in camera hearing and shall be furnished to the Arkansas Supreme Court on appeal.

(C) If, following the hearing, the court determines that the offered proof is relevant to a fact in issue, and that its probative value outweighs its inflammatory or prejudicial nature, the court shall make a written order stating what evidence, if any, may be introduced by the defendant and the nature of the question to be permitted in accordance with the applicable rules of evidence.

(3)(A) If the court determines that some or all of the offered proof is relevant to a fact in issue, the victim shall be told of the court's order and given the opportunity to consult in private with the prosecuting attorney.

(B) If the prosecuting attorney is satisfied that the order substantially prejudices the prosecution of the case, an interlocutory appeal on behalf of the state may be taken in accordance with

Rule 36.10(a) and (c)

MISCELLANEOUS STATE STATUTES

CALIFORNIA

▫ Cal. Penal Code

Chapter 1 Rape, Abduction, Carnal
Abuse of Children, and Seduction

§261. Rape Defined

(a) Rape is an act of sexual intercourse accomplished with a person not the spouse of the perpetrator, under any of the following circumstances:

(1) Where a person is incapable, because of a mental disorder or developmental or physical disability, of giving legal consent, and this is known or reasonably should be known to the person committing the act. Notwithstanding the existence of a conservatorship pursuant to the provisions of the Lanterman-Petris-Short Act (Part 1 (commencing with Section 5000) of Division 5 of the welfare and Institutions Code), the prosecuting attorney shall prove, as an element of the crime, that a mental disorder or developmental or physical disability rendered the alleged victim incapable of giving consent.

(2) Where it is accomplished against a person's will by means of force, violence, duress, menace, or fear of immediate and unlawful bodily injury on the person or another.

(3) Where a person is prevented from resisting by any intoxicating or anesthetic substance, or any controlled substance,

administered by or with the privity of the accused.

(4) Where a person is at the time unconscious of the nature of the act, and this is known to the accused.

(5) Where a person submits under the belief that the person committing the act is the victim's spouse, and this belief is induced by any artifice, pretense, or concealment practiced by the accused, with intent to induce the belief.

(6) Where the act is accomplished against the victim's will by threatening to retaliate in the future against the victim or any other person, and there is a reasonable possibility that the perpetrator will execute the threat. As used in this paragraph "threatening to retaliate" means a threat to kidnap or falsely imprison, or to inflict extreme pain, serious bodily injury, or death.

(7) Where the act is accomplished against the victim's will by threatening to use the authority of a public official to incarcerate, arrest, or deport the victim or another, and the victim has a reasonable belief that the perpetrator is a public official. As used in this paragraph, "public official" means a person employed by a governmental agency who has the authority, as part of that position, to incarcerate, arrest, or deport another. The perpetrator does not actually have to be a public official

(b) As used in this section, "duress" means a direct or implied threat of force, violence, danger, hardship, or retribution sufficient to coerce a reasonable person of ordinary susceptibilities to perform an act which otherwise would not have been performed, or acquiesce in an act to which one otherwise would not have submitted. The total circumstances, including the age of the victim, and his or her relationship to the defendant, are factors to consider in appraising the existence of duress.

(c) As used in this section, "menace" means any threat, declaration, or act which shows an intention to inflict an injury upon another.

§261.6 Consent, defined; current or previous dating relationship; admissibility of evidence; burden of proof

In prosecutions under §§ 261, 288a, or 289, in which consent is at issue, "consent" shall be defined to mean positive cooperation in act or attitude pursuant to an exercise of free will. The person must act freely and voluntarily and have knowledge of the nature of the act or transaction involved.

A current or previous dating relationship shall not be sufficient to constitute consent where consent is at issue in a prosecution under §§ 261, 286, 288a or 289.

Nothing in this section shall affect the admissibility of evidence or the burden of proof on the issue of consent.

RAPE

§262. Rape of Spouse

(a) Rape of a person who is the spouse of a perpetrator is an act of sexual intercourse accomplished against the will of the spouse by means of force or fear of immediate and unlawful bodily injury on the spouse or another, or where the act is accomplished against the victim's will by threatening to retaliate in the future against the victim or any other person, and there is a reasonable possibility that the perpetrator will execute the threat. As used in this subdivision "threatening to retaliate" means a threat to kidnap of falsely imprison, or to inflict extreme pain, serious bodily injury, or death.

(b) the provisions of Section 800 shall apply to this section; however, there shall be no arrest or prosecution under this section unless the violation of this section is reported to a peace officer having the power to arrest for a violation of this section or to the district attorney of the county in which the violation occurred, within 90 days after the day of the violation.

§263. Rape; essentials; sufficiency of penetration

The essential guilt of rape consists in the outrage to the person and feelings of the victim of rape. Any sexual penetration, however slight, is sufficient to complete the crime.

§264. Rape; rape of spouse; unlawful sexual intercourse; punishment

(a) Rape, as defined in Section 261, is punishable by imprisonment in the state prison for three, six or eight years. Rape, as defined in Section 262, is punishable either by imprisonment in the county jail for not more that one year or in the state prison for three, six or eight years. Unlawful sexual intercourse, as defined in Section 261.5, is punishable either by imprisonment in the county jail for not more that one year or in the state prison.

(b) In addition to any punishment imposed under this section, the judge may assess a fine not to exceed seventy dollars ($70) against any person who violates Section 261, 261.5, or 262 with the proceeds of this fine to be used in accordance with Section 1463.23. The court shall, however, take into consideration the defendant's ability to pay, and no defendant shall be denied probation because of his or her inability to pay the fine permitted under this subdivision.

COLORADO

□ **Colo. Rev. Stat. Ann.
Criminal Code**

§18-3-401. Definitions. (2) "Intimate parts" means the external genitalia or the perineum or the anus or the pubes or the breast of any person.

(2.5) "Pattern of sexual abuse" means the commission of two or more incidents of sexual contact involving a child when such offenses are committed by an actor upon the same victim.

(3.5) One in a "position of trust" includes, but is not limited to, amu person who is a parent or acting in the place of a parent and charged with any of the parent's rights, duties, or responsibilities concerning a child, including a guardian or someone otherwise responsible for the general supervision of a child's welfare, or a person who is charged with any duty or responsibility for the health, education, welfare, or supervision of child, including foster care, child care, family care, or institutional care, either independently or through another, no matter how brief, at the time of an unlawful act.

(4) "Sexual contact" means the knowingly touching of the victim's intimate parts by the actor, or of the actor's intimate parts by the victim, of the knowingly touching of the clothing covering the immediate area of the victim's or actor's intimate parts if that sexual contact can reasonably be construed as being for the purposes of sexual arousal, gratification, or abuse.

(5) "Sexual intrusion" means any intrusion, however slight, by any object or any part of a person's body, except the mouth, tongue, or penis, into the genital or anal opening of another person's body if that sexual intrusion can reasonably be construed as being for the purposes of sexual arousal, gratification, or abuse.

(6) "Sexual penetration" means sexual intercourse, cunnilingus, fellatio, analingus, or anal intercourse. Emission need not be proved as an element of any sexual penetration. Any penetration, however slight, is sufficient to complete the crime.

(7) "Victim" means the person alleging to have been subjected to a criminal sexual assault.

§18-3-406. Criminality of conduct. (1) If the criminality of conduct depends on a child's being below the age of eighteen and the child was in fact at least fifteen years of age, it shall be an affirmative defense that the defendant reasonably believed the child to be eighteen years of age or older.

(2) If the criminality of conduct depends upon a child being below the age of fifteen, it shall be no defense that the defendant did not know the child's age or that he reasonably believed the child to be fifteen years of age or older.

§18-3-4-7. Victim's prior history - evidentiary hearing. (1) Evidence of specific instances of the victim's prior or subsequent sexual conduct, opinion evidence of the victim's sexual conduct, reputation evidence of the victim's sexual conduct shall be presumed to be irrelevant except:

    (a) Evidence of the victim's prior or subsequent sexual conduct with the actor;

    (b) Evidence of specific instances of sexual activity showing the source or origin of semen, pregnancy, disease, or any similar evidence of sexual intercourse offered for the purpose of showing that the act or acts charged were or were not committed by the defendant.

(2) In any criminal prosecution under §§ 18-3-402 to 18-3-405, or for attempt or conspiracy to commit any crime under §§ 18-3-402 to 18-3-405, if evidence, which is not excepted under subsection(1) of this section, of specific instances of the victim's prior or subsequent sexual conduct, or opinion evidence of the victim's sexual conduct, or evidence that the victim has a history of false reporting of sexual assaults is to be offered at trial, the following procedure shall be followed:

(a) A written motion shall be made at least thirty days prior to trial, unless later for good cause shown, to the court and to the opposing parties stating that the moving part has an offer of proof of the relevancy and materiality of evidence of specific instances of the victim's prior or subsequent sexual conduct, or opinion evidence of the victim's sexual conduct, or reputation evidence of the victim's sexual conduct, or evidence that the victim has a history of false reporting of sexual assaults which is proposed to be presented.

(b) The written motion shall be accompanied by an affidavit in which the offer of proof shall be stated.

(c) If the court finds that offer of proof is sufficient. the court shall notify the other party of such and set a hearing to be held in camera prior to trial. In such hearing, the court shall allow the questioning of the victim regarding the offer of proof made by the moving party and shall otherwise allow a full presentation of the offer of proof including, but not limited to, the presentation of witnesses.

(d) An in camera hearing may be held during trial if evidence first becomes available at the time of the trial or for good cause shown.

(e) At the conclusion of the hearing, if the court finds that the evidence proposed to be offered regarding the sexual conduct of the victim is relevant to a material issue to the case, the court shall order that evidence may be introduced and prescribe the nature of the evidence or question to be permitted. The moving party may then offer evidence pursuant to the order of the court.

§18-3-408. Jury instruction prohibited. In any criminal prosecution under §§ 18-3-402 to 18-3-405, or for an attempt or conspiracy to commit any crime under §§ 18-3-402 to 18-3-405, the jury shall not be instructed to examine with caution the testimony of the victim solely because of the nature of the charge, nor shall the jury be instructed that such charge is easy to make but difficult to defend against, nor shall any similar instruction be given. However, the jury shall be instructed not to allow gender bias or any kind of prejudice based upon gender to influence the decision of the jury.

§18-3-409. Marital defense. Any marital relationship, whether established statutorily, putatively, or by common law, between an actor and victim shall not be a defense to any offense under this part 4 unless such defense is specifically set forth in the applicable statutory section by having the elements of the offense specifically exclude a spouse.

DELAWARE

□ De. Code Ann.

Subpart D. Sexual Offenses

§761. Definitions generally applicable to sexual offenses.

(a) "Cunnilingus" means any oral contact with the female genitalia.

(b) "Fellatio" means any oral contact with the male genitalia.

(c) "Object" means any item, device, instrument, substance or part of the body other than a tongue or penis. It does not mean a medical instrument used by a licensed medical doctor or nurse for the purpose of diagnosis or treatment.

(d) "Sexual offense" means any offense defined by §§ 761-775 and 1109 of this title.

(e) "Sexual intercourse" means:

(1) Any act of physical union of the genitalia or anus of 1 person with the mouth, anus or genitalia of another person. It occurs upon any penetration, however slight. Ejaculation is not required. This offense encompasses the

crime commonly known as rape and sodomy; or

(f) "Sexual contact" means any intentional touching of the anus, breast, buttocks or genitalia of another person and shall also include touching of those specified areas when covered by clothing.

(g) "Without consent" means:

(1) The defendant compelled the victim to submit by force, by gesture, or by threat of death, physical injury, pain or kidnapping to be inflicted upon the victim or a third party, or by any other means which would compel a reasonable person under the circumstances to submit. It is not required that the victim resist such force or threat to the utmost, or to resist if resistance would be futile or foolhardy, but the victim need resist only to the extent that is reasonably necessary to make the victim's refusal to consent known to the defendant; or

(2) The defendant knew that the victim was unconscious, asleep or otherwise unaware that a sexual act was being performed;

§770. Unlawful sexual penetration in the third degree; class D felony.

(a) A person is guilty of unlawful sexual penetration n the third degree when he intentionally places 1 or more fingers or thumbs or an object, as defined by §761(c) of this title, insider the vagina or anus of a person under any of the following circumstances:

(1) The sexual penetration without the victim's consent; or

(2) The victim is less than 16 years old.

(b) This law does not apply to a licensed medical doctor or nurse who places 1 or more fingers or an object inside a vagina or anus for the purpose of diagnosis or treatment.

§771. Unlawful sexual penetration in the second degree; class C felony.

A person is guilty of unlawful sexual penetration in the second degree when he intentionally places 1 or more fingers or thumbs or an object, as defined by §761(c) of this title, inside the vagina or anus of a person under any of the following circumstances:

(1) The sexual penetration occurs without the victim's consent and during the commission of the crime, or during the immediate flight from the crime, he causes physical injury to the victim; or

(2) The victim is less than 16 years old and during the commission of the crime, or during the immediate flight from the crime, or during an attempt to prevent the reporting of the crime, he causes physical injury to the victim.

§772. Unlawful sexual penetration in the first degree; class B felony.

A person is guilty of an unlawful penetration in the first degree when he intentionally places 1 or more fingers or thumbs or an object, as defined by §761(c) of this title, inside the vagina or anus of a person under any of the following circumstances:

(1) The sexual penetration occurs without the victim's consent and during the commission of the

crime, or during the immediate flight from the crime, or during an attempt to prevent the reporting of the crime, he causes serious physical injury to the victim; or

(2) The victim is less than 16 years old and during the commission of the crime, or during the immediate flight from the crime, or during an attempt to prevent the reporting of the crime, he causes serious physical injury to the victim; or

(3) The sexual penetration occurs without the victim's consent and during the commission of the crime or during the immediate flight from the crime, or during an attempt to prevent the reporting of the crime, he displays what appears to be a deadly weapon or dangerous instrument; or

(4) The victim is less than 16 years old and during the commission of the crime, or during the immediate flight form the crime, or during an attempt to prevent the reporting of the crime, he displays what appears to be a deadly weapon or a dangerous instrument.

§775. Unlawful sexual intercourse in the first degree; class A felony.

(a) A person is guilty of unlawful sexual intercourse in the first degree when he intentionally engages in sexual intercourse with another person and any of the following circumstances exist:

(1) The intercourse occurs without the victim's consent, and he inflicts serious physical, mental or emotional injury upon the victim:

RAPE

    a. On the occasion of the crime; or

    b. During the immediate flight from the crime; or

    c. During an attempt to prevent the reporting of the crime; or

(2) The intercourse occurs without the victim's consent and the defendant was not the victim's voluntary social companion on the occasion of the crime and had not permitted the defendant sexual intercourse within the previous 12 months; or

(3) In the course of committing unlawful sexual intercourse in the third degree or unlawful sexual intercourse in the second degree, the defendant displayed what appeared to be a deadly weapon or a dangerous instrument; or

(4) The victim is less than 16 years of age and the defendant is not the victim's voluntary social companion on the occasion of the crime.

(b) Nothing contained in this section shall preclude a separate charge, conviction and sentence for possession of a deadly weapon during the commission of a felony.

Unlawful sexual intercourse in the first degree is a class A felony.

MISCELLANEOUS STATE STATUTES

DISTRICT OF COLUMBIA

◻ D.S. Code Ann.

CHAPTER 28. RAPE.

§22-2801. Definition and penalty.

Whoever has carnal knowledge of a female forcibly and against her will or whoever carnally knows and abuses a female child under 16 years of age, shall be imprisoned for any term of years or for life. (Mar. 3, 1901, 31 Stat.)

FLORIDA

◻ Fla. Stat. Ann.

CHAPTER 794
SEXUAL BATTERY

§794.011. Sexual Battery

(1) Definitions:

(a) The term " consent" means intelligent, knowing, and voluntary consent and shall not be construed to include coerced submission.

(b) The term "mentally defective" means that a person suffers from a mental disease or defect which renders that person temporarily or permanently incapable of appraising the nature of his or her conduct.

(c) The term "mentally incapacitated" means that a person is rendered temporarily incapable of appraising or controlling his or her conduct due to the influence of a narcotic, anesthetic, or intoxicating substance administered to that person without his or her consent or due to any other act committed upon that person without his or her consent.

(d) The term "offender" means a person accused of a sexual offense.

(e) The term "physically helpless" means that a person is unconscious, asleep, or for any other reason physically unable to communicate unwillingness to an act.

(f) The term "retaliation" includes, but is not limited to, threats of future physical punishment, kidnapping, false imprisonment or forcible confinement, or extortion.

(g) The term "serious personal injury" means great bodily harm or pain, permanent disability or permanent disfigurement.

(h) The term "sexual battery" means oral, anal, or vaginal penetration by, or union with, the sexual organ of another or the anal or vaginal penetration of another by any other object; however, sexual battery does not include an act done for a bona fide medical purpose.

(i) The term "victim" means the person alleging to have been the object of a sexual offense.

(j) The term "physically incapacitated" means that a person is bodily impaired or handicapped and substantially limited in his or her ability to resist or flee an act.

(2) A person 18 years of age or older who commits sexual battery upon, or injures the sexual organs of, a person less than 12 years of age in an attempt to commit sexual battery upon such person commits a capital felony, punishable as provided in § 775.082 and 921.141. If the offender is under the age of 18, that person is guilty of a life felony, punishable as provided in § 775.082, § 775.083, or § 775.084.

(4) A person who commits sexual battery upon a person 12 years of age or older, without the person's consent, under any of the following circumstances is guilty of a felony of the first degree, punishable as provided in § 775.082, § 775.083, or § 775.084:

(a) When the victim is physically helpless to resist.

(b) When the offender coerces the victim to submit by threatening to use force or violence likely to cause serious personal injury on the victim, and the victim reasonably believes that the offender has the present ability to execute the threat.

(c) When the offender coerces the victim to submit by threatening to retaliate against the victim, or any other person, and the victim reasonably believes that the offender has the ability to execute the threat in the future.

(d) When the offender, without the prior knowledge or consent of the victim, administers, or has knowledge of someone else administering to the victim any narcotic, anesthetic, or other intoxicating substance which mentally or physically incapacitates the victim.

(e) When the victim is mentally defective and the offender has reason to believe this or has actual knowledge of this fact.

(f) When the victim is physically incapacitated.

(5) A person who commits sexual battery upon a person 12 years of age or older, without that person's consent, and in the process thereof uses physical force and violence not likely to cause serious personal injury is guilty of a felony of the second degree, punishable as provided in § 775.082, § 775.084.

(6) Evidence of the victim's mental incapacity or defect is admissible to prove that the consent was not intelligent, knowing or voluntary; and the court shall instruct the jury accordingly.

§794.05 Carnal intercourse with unmarried person under 18 years

(1) Any person who has unlawful carnal intercourse with any unmarried person, of previous chaste character, who at the time of such intercourse is under the age of 18 years, shall be guilty of a felony

of the second degree, punishable as provided in §§ 775.082, 775.083, or 775.084.

(2) It shall not be a defense to a prosecution under this section that the prosecuting witness was not of previous chaste character at the time of the act when the lack of previous chaste character in the prosecuting witness was caused solely by previous intercourse between the defendant and the prosecuting.

§794.021 Ignorance or belief as to victim's age no defense

When, in this chapter, the criminality of conduct depends upon the victim's being below a certain specified age, ignorance of the age is no defense. Neither shall misrepresentation of age by such person nor a bona fide belief that such person is over the specified age be a defense.

§794.022 Rules of evidence

(1) The testimony of the victim need not be corroborated in prosecutions under §794.011, however, the court may instruct the jury with respect to the weight and quality of the evidence.

(2) Specific instances of prior consensual sexual activity between the victim and any person other than the offender shall not be admitted into evidence in prosecutions under §794.021; however, when consent by the victim is at issue, such evidence may be admitted if it is first established to the court outside the presence of the jury that such activity shows such a relation to the conduct involved in the case that it tends to establish a

pattern of conduct or behavior on the part of the victim which is relevant to the issue of consent.

IDAHO

◻ Idaho Code

CHAPTER
RAPE

§18-6101. Rape defined. - Rape is an act of sexual intercourse accomplished with a female under either of the following circumstances:

1. Where the female is under the age of eighteen (18) years.

2. Where she is incapable through lunacy or any other unsoundness of mind, whether temporary or permanent, of giving legal consent.

3. Where she resists but her resistance is overcome by force or violence.

4. Where she is prevented from resistance by threats of immediate and great bodily harm, accompanied by apparent power of execution; or by any intoxicating narcotic, or anaesthetic substance administered by or with the privity of the accused.

5. Where she is at the time unconscious of the nature of the act, and this is known to the accused.

6. Where she submits under the belief that the person committing the act is her husband, and the belief is induced by artifice, pretense or concealment practiced by the accused, with intent to induce such belief.

§18-6102. Proof of physical ability. - no conviction for rape can be had against one who was under the age of fourteen (14) years at the time of the act alleged, unless his physical ability to accomplish penetration is proved as an independent fact, and beyond a reasonable doubt.

§18-6103. Penetration. - The essential guilt of rape consists in the outrage to the person and feelings of the female. Any sexual penetration, however slight, is sufficient to complete the crime.

§18-6104. Punishment for rape. - Rape is punishable by imprisonment in the state prison not less than one (1) year, and the imprisonment may be extended to life in the discretion of the District Judge, who shall pass sentence.

§18-6105. Evidence of previous sexual conduct of prosecuting witness.- In prosecutions for the crime of rape, evidence of the prosecuting witness' previous sexual conduct shall not be admitted nor reference made thereto in the presence of the jury, except as provided hereinafter. The defendant may make application to the court before or during the trial for the admission of evidence concerning the previous sexual conduct of the prosecuting witness. Upon such application the court shall conduct a hearing out of the presence of the jury as to the relevancy of such evidence of previous sexual conduct and shall limit the questioning and control the admission and exclusion of evidence upon trial. Nothing in this section shall limit the right of either the state or the accused to impeach credibility by the showing of prior felony convictions.

§18-6107.   Rape of spouse. - No person shall be convicted of rape for any acts with that person's spouse, except under the circumstances cited in paragraphs 3. and 4. of § 18-6101, Idaho Code.

§18-6108.   Male rape. - Male rape is defined as the penetration, however slight, of the oral or anal opening of another male, with the perpetrator's penis, for the purpose of sexual arousal, gratification or abuse, under any of the following circumstances:

1. Where the victim is incapable, through lunacy or any other unsoundness of mind, whether temporary or permanent, of giving consent.

2. Where the victim resists but his resistance is overcome by force or violence.

3. Where the victim is prevented from resistance by the use of any intoxicating, narcotic, or anaesthetic substance administered by or with the privity of the accused.

4. Where the victim is at the time unconscious of the mature of the act, and this is known to the accused.

ILLINOIS

□ Ill. Ann. Stat. (Smith-Hurd)

Criminal sexual assault

Criminal Sexual Assault. (a) The accused commits criminal sexual assault if he or she:

(1) commits an act of sexual penetration by the use of force or threat of force; or

(2) commits an act of sexual penetration and the accused know that the victim was unable to understand the nature of the act or was unable to give knowing consent;or

(3) commits an act of sexual penetration with a victim who was under 18 years of age when the act was committed and the accused was a family member; or

(4) commits an act of sexual penetration with a victim who was at least 13 years of age but under 18 years of age when the act was committed and the accused was 17 years of age or over and held a position of trust, authority or supervision in relation to the victim.

(b) Sentence. Criminal sexual assault is a Class 2 felony. A second or subsequent conviction for a violation of this Section or under any similar statute of this State or any other state for any offense involving criminal sexual assault prohibited under this Section is a Class X felony. When a person has any such prior conviction, the information or indictment charging that person shall state such prior conviction so as to give notice of the State's intention to treat the charge as a Class X felony. The fact of such prior conviction is not an element of the offense and may not be disclosed to the jury during trial unless otherwise permitted by issues properly raised during such trial.

§12-14. Aggravated criminal sexual assault

§12-14. Aggravated Criminal Sexual Assault. (a) The accused commits aggravated criminal sexual assault if he or she commits criminal sexual assault and any of the following aggravating circumstances existed during the commission of the offense:

> (1) the accused displayed, threatened to use, or used a dangerous weapon or any object fashioned or utilized in such a manner as to lead the victim under the circumstances reasonably to believe it to be a dangerous weapon; or

> (2) the accused caused bodily harm to the victim; or

> (3) the accused acted in such a manner as to threatened or endanger the life of the victim or any other person; or

> (4) the criminal sexual assault was perpetrated during the course of the commission or attempted commission of any other felony by the accused; or

(5) the victim was 60 years of age or over when the offense was committed; or

(6) the victim was a physically handicapped person.

(b) The accused commits aggravated criminal sexual assault if:

(1) the accused was 17 years of age and (i) commits and act of sexual penetration with a victim who was under 13 years of age when the act was committed; or

(2) the accused was under 17 years of age and (i) commits an act of sexual penetration with a victim who was under 9 years of age when the act was committed; or (ii) commits an act of sexual penetration with a victim who was at least 9 years of age but under 13 years of age when the act was committed and the accused used force or threat of force to commit the act.

(c) The accused commits aggravated criminal sexual assault if he or she commits an act of sexual penetration with a victim who was an institutionalized severely or profoundly mentally retarded at the time the act was committed.

§12-15. Criminal sexual abuse

§12-15. Criminal Sexual Abuse. (a) The accused commits criminal sexual abuse if he or she:

(1) commits an act of sexual conduct by the use of force or threat of force;

(2) commits an act of sexual conduct and the accused knew that the victim was unable to understand the nature of the act or was unable to give knowing consent.

(b) The accused commits criminal sexual abuse if the accused was under 17 years of age and commits an act of sexual abuse if the accused was under 17 years of age and commits an act of sexual penetration or sexual conduct with a victim who was at least 9 years of age but under 17 years of age when the act was committed.

(c) The accused commits criminal sexual abuse if he or she commits an act of sexual penetration or sexual conduct with a victim who was at least 13 years of age but under 17 years of age and the accused was less than 5 years older than the victim.

(d) Sentence. Criminal sexual abuse is a Class A misdemeanor. A second or subsequent conviction for a violation of subsection (a) of this Section is a Class 2 felony. for purposes of this Section, it is a second or subsequent conviction if the accused has at any time been convicted under this Section or under any similar statute of this State or any other state for any offense involving sexual abuse or sexual assault that is substantially equivalent to or more serious than the sexual abuse prohibited under this Section.

§12-16.2 Criminal transmission of HIV

§12-16.2 Criminal Transmission of HIV. (a) A person commits criminal transmission of HIV when he or she, knowing that he or she is infected with HIV:

(1) engages in intimate contact with another;

(2) transfers, donates, or provides his or her blood, tissue, semen, organs, or their potentially infectious body fluids for transfusion, transplantation, insemination, or other administration to another; or

(3) dispenses, delivers, exchanges, sells, or in any other way transfers to another any nonsterile intravenous or intramuscular drug paraphernalia.

(b) For purposes of this Section:

"HIV" means the human immunodeficiency virus or any other identified causative agent of acquired immunodeficiency syndrome.

"Intimate contact with another" means the exposure of the body of one person to a bodily fluid of another person in a manner that could result in the transmission of HIV.

"Intravenous or intramuscular drug paraphernalia" means any equipment, product, or material of any kind which is peculiar to and marketed for use in injecting a substance into the human body.

(c) Nothing in this Section shall be construed to require that an infection with HIV has occurred in order for a person to have committed criminal transmission of HIV.

(d) It shall be an affirmative defense that the person exposed knew that the infected person was infected with HIV, knew that the action could result in infection with HIV, and consented to the action with that knowledge.

(e) A person who commits criminal transmission of HIV commits a Class 2 felony.

KANSAS

◻ **Kan. Stat. Ann.**

Article 35. SEX OFFENSES

Law Review and Bar Journal References: "Survey of Kansas Law: Criminal Law," Robert A. Waterson, 32 K.L.R. 395(1984).

§21-3501. Definitions. The following definitions apply in this article unless a different meaning is plainly required:

(1) Sexual intercourse: means any penetration of the female sex organ by a finger, the male sex organ or any object. Any penetration, however slight, is sufficient to constitute sexual intercourse. "Sexual intercourse" does not include penetration of the female sex organ by a finger or object in the course of the performance of:

(a) Generally recognized health care practices; or

(b) a body cavity search conducted in accordance with K.S.A. §§ 22-2520 through 22-2523, and amendments thereto.

(2) "Sodomy" means oral or anal copulation; oral or anal copulation or sexual intercourse between a person and an animal; or any penetration of the anal opening by any body part or object. Any penetration, however slight is sufficient to constitute sodomy. "sodomy" does not include penetration of the anal opening by a finger or object in the course of the performance of:

(a) Generally recognized health care practices; or

(b) a body cavity search conducted in accordance with Kansas Statutes Annotated §§ 22-2520 through 22-2524, and amendments thereto.

(3) "spouse" means a lawful husband or wife, unless the couple is living apart in separate residences or either spouse has filed an action for annulment, separate maintenance or divorce or for relief under the protection from abuse act.

(4) "Unlawful sexual act" means any rape, indecent liberties with a child, aggravated indecent liberties with a child, criminal sodomy, aggravated criminal sodomy, lewd and lascivious behavior, sexual battery or aggravated sexual battery, as defined in this code.

§21-3502. Rape. (1) Rape is sexual intercourse with a person who does not consent to the sexual intercourse, under any of the following circumstances:

(a) When the victim is overcome by force or fear;

(b) when the victim is unconscious or physically powerless;

(c) when the victim is incapable of giving consent because of mental deficiency or disease, which condition was known by the offender or was reasonably apparent to the offender; or

(d) when the victim is incapable of giving consent because of the effect of any alcoholic liquor, narcotic, drug or other substance administered to the victim by the offender, or by another person with the offender's knowledge, unless the victim voluntarily consumes or allows the administration of the substance with knowledge of its nature.

(2) Rape is a class B felony.

MAINE

◻ Me. Stat. Ann.

CHAPTER 11
SEX OFFENSES

§251. Definitions and general provisions

1. In this chapter the following definitions apply.

MISCELLANEOUS STATE STATUTES

A. "Spouse" means a person legally married to the actor, but does not include a legally married person living apart from the actor under a defacto separation.

B. "Sexual intercourse" means any penetration of the female sex organ by the male sex organ. Emissions is not required.

C. "Sexual act" means any act of sexual gratification between 2 persons involving direct physical contact between the sex organs of one and the mouth or anus of the other or direct physical contact between the sex organs of one and the sex organs of the other, or direct physical contact between the sex organs of one and an instrument or device manipulated by the other. A sexual act may be proved without allegation or proof of penetration.

D. "Sexual contact" means any touching of the genitals directly or through clothing, other than as would constitute a sexual act, for the purpose of arousing or gratifying sexual desire.

E. "Compulsion" means physical force, a threat of physical force or a combination thereof which makes a person unable to physically repel the actor or which produces in that person a reasonable fear that death, serious bodily injury or kidnapping might be imminently inflicted upon that person or upon another human being.

§253. Gross sexual assault

1. A person is guilty of gross sexual assault if that person engages in a sexual act with another person and:

RAPE

A. The other person submits as a result of compulsion, as defined in § 251, subsection 1, paragraph E; or

B. The other person, not the actor's spouse, has not in fact attained the age of 14 years.

2. A person is guilty of gross sexual assault if that person engages in a sexual act with another person and:

A. The actor has substantially impaired the other person's power to appraise or control the other person's sexual acts by administering or employing drugs, intoxicants or other similar means;

B. The actor compels or induces the other person to engage in the sexual act by any threat;

C. The other person suffers from mental disability that is reasonably apparent or known to the actor, and which in fact renders the other person substantially incapable of appraising the nature of the contact involved or of understanding that the person has the right to deny or with draw consent;

D. The other person is unconscious or otherwise physically incapable of resisting and has not consented to the sexual act;

E. The other person, not the actor's spouse, is in official custody as a probationer or as a parolee, or is detained in a hospital, prison or other institution, and the actor has supervisory or disciplinary authority over the other person.

MINNESOTA

◻ **Minn. Stat. Ann.**

§609.341 Definitions

Subdivision 1. For the purposes of §§ 609.341 to 609.351, the terms in this section have the meanings given them.

Subd. 2. "Actor" means a person accused of criminal sexual conduct.

Subd. 3. "Force" means the infliction, attempted infliction, or threatened infliction by the actor of bodily harm or commission or threat of any other crime by the actor against the complainant or another, which (a) causes the complainant to reasonably believe that the actor has the present ability to execute the threat and (b) if the actor does not have a significant relationship to the complainant, also causes the complainant to submit.

Subd. 4. "Consent" means a voluntary uncoerced manifestation of a present agreement to perform a particular sexual act with the actor.

Subd. 5. "Intimate parts" includes the primary genital area, groin, inner thigh, buttocks or breast of a human being.

Subd. 6. "Mentally impaired" means that person, as a result of inadequately developed or impaired intelligence or a substantial psychiatric disorder of thought or mood, lacks the judgement to give a reasoned consent to sexual contact or to sexual penetration.

Subd. 7. "Mentally incapacitated" means that a person under the influence of alcohol, a narcotic, anesthetic, or any other substance, administered to that person without the person's agreement, lacks the judgment to give a reasoned consent to sexual contact or sexual penetration.

Subd. 8. "Personal injury" means bodily harm as defined in § 609.02, subdivision 7, or severe mental anguish or pregnancy.

Subd. 9. "Physically helpless" means that a person is (a) asleep or not conscious, (b) unable to withhold consent or to withdraw because of a physical condition, or (c) unable to communicate nonconsent and the condition is known or reasonably should have been known to the actor.

Subd. 10. "Position of authority" includes but is not limited to any person who is a parent or acting in the place of a parent and charged with any of a parent's rights, duties or responsibilities to a child, or a person who is charged with any duty or responsibility for the health, welfare, or supervision of a child, either independently or through another, no matter how brief, at the time of the act.

Subd. 11. (a) "Sexual contact," for the purposes of § 609.343, subdivision 1, clauses (a) to (f), and

§609.345, subdivision 1, clauses (a) to (e), and (h) to (k), includes any of the following acts committed with out the complainant's consent, except in those cases where consent is not a defense, and committed with sexual or aggressive intent:

(i) the intentional touching by the actor of the complainant's intimate parts, or

(ii) the touching by the complainant of the actor's, the complainant's, or another's intimate parts effected by coercion or the use of a position of authority, or by inducement if the complainant is under 13 years of age or mentally impaired, or

(iii) the touching by another of the complainant's intimate parts effected by coercion or the use of a position of authority, or

(iv) in any of the cases above, the touching of the clothing covering the immediate area of the intimate parts.

(b) "Sexual contact," for the purposes of §§ 609.343, subdivision 1, clauses (g) and (h), and §609.345, subdivision 1, clauses (f) and (g), includes any of the following acts committed with sexual or aggressive intent:

(i) the intentional touching by the actor of the complainant's intimate parts;

(ii) the touching by the complainant of the actor's, the complainant's, or another's intimate parts;

(iii) the touching by another of the complainant's intimate parts; or

(iv) in any of the cases listed above, touching of the clothing covering the immediate area of the intimate parts.

609.342. Criminal sexual conduct in the first degree

Subdivision 1. Crime defined. A person who engages in sexual penetration with another person is guilty of criminal sexual conduct in the first degree if any of the following circumstances exists:

(a) the complainant is under 13 years of age and the actor is more than 36 months older than the complainant. Neither mistake as to the complainant's age nor consent to the act by the complainant is a defense;

(b) the complainant is at least 13 but less than 16 years of age and the actor is more than 48 months older than the complainant and in a position of authority over the complainant, and uses this authority to cause the complainant to submit. Neither mistake as to the complainant's age nor consent to the act by the complainant is a defense;

(c) circumstances existing at the time of the act cause the complainant to have a reasonable fear of imminent great bodily harm to the complainant or another;

(d) the actor is armed with a dangerous weapon or any article used or fashioned in a manner to lead the complainant to reasonably believe it to be a dangerous weapon and uses or threatens to use the weapon or article to cause the complainant to submit;

(e) the actor causes person injury to the complainant, and either of the following circumstances exist:

(i) the actor or an accomplice used force or coercion to accomplish the penetration;

(ii) the actor or an accomplice was armed with a dangerous weapon or any article used or fashioned in a manner to lead the complainant to reasonably believe it could be a dangerous weapon and used or threatened to use the dangerous weapon;

(iii) circumstances existed at the time of the act to cause the complainant to have a reasonable fear of imminent great bodily harm to the complainant or another;

(iv) the complainant suffered personal injury; or

(v) the sexual abuse involved multiple acts committed over an extended period of time.

Neither mistake as to the complainant's age not consent to the act by the complainant is a defense.

Subd. 2. Penalty. A person convicted under subdivision 1 may be sentenced to imprisonment for not more than 20 years or to a payment of a fine of not more than $35,000, or both.

Subd. 3. Stay. Except when imprisonment is required under § 609.346, if a person is convicted under subdivision 1, clause (g), the court may stay imposition or execution of the sentence if it finds that:

> (a) a stay is in the best interest of the complainant or the family unit; and

> (b) a professional assessment indicates that the offender has been accepted by and can respond to a treatment program.

If the court stays imposition or execution of sentence, it shall include the following as conditions of probation:

> (1) incarceration in a local jail or workhouse; and

> (2) a requirement that the offender complete a treatment program

609.347. Evidence

Subd. 1. In a prosecution under §§ 609.342 to 609.346, the testimony of a victim need not be corroborated.

MISCELLANEOUS STATE STATUTES

Subd. 2. In a prosecution under §§ 609.342 to 609.346, there is no need to show that the victim resisted the accused.

Subd. 3. In a prosection under §§ 609.342 to 609.346 or 609.365, evidence of the victim's previous sexual conduct shall not be admitted not shall any reference to such conduct be made in the presence of the jury, except by court order under the procedure provided in subdivision 4. The evidence can be admitted only if the probative value of the evidence is not substantially outweighed by its inflammatory or prejudicial nature and only in the circumstances set out in paragraphs (a) and (b). for the evidence to be admissible under paragraph (a), subsection (i), the judge must find by a preponderance of the evidence that the facts set out in the accused's offer of proof are true. For the evidence to be admissible under paragraph (a), subsection (ii) or paragraph (b), the judge must find that the evidence is sufficient to support a finding that the facts set out in the accused's offer of proof are true, as provided under Rule 901 of the Rules of Evidence.

(a) When consent of the victim is a defense in the case, the following evidence is admissible:

(i) evidence of the victim's previous sexual conduct tending to establish a common scheme or plan of similar sexual conduct under circumstances similar to the case at issue. In order to find a common scheme or plan, the judge must find that the victim made prior allegations of sexual assault which were fabricated; and

(ii) evidence of the victim's previous sexual conduct with the accused.

(b) When the prosecution's case includes evidence of semen, pregnancy, or disease at the time of the incident or, in the case of pregnancy, between the time of the incident and trial, evidence of specific instances of the victim's previous sexual conduct is admissible solely to show the source of the semen, pregnancy, or disease.

Subd. 4.   The accused may not offer evidence described in subdivision 3 except pursuant to the following procedure:

(a) A motion shall be made by the accused at least three business days prior to trial. unless later for good cause shown, setting out with particularity the offer of proof of the evidence that the accused intends to offer, relative to the previous sexual conduct of the victim;

(b) If the court deems the offer of proof sufficient, the court shall order a hearing out of the presence of the jury, if any, and in such hearing shall allow the accused to make a full presentation of the offer of proof;

(c) At the conclusion of the hearing, if the court finds that the evidence proposed to be offered by the accused regarding the previous sexual conduct of the victim is admissible under subdivision 3 and that its probative value is not substantially outweighed by its inflammatory or prejudicial nature, the court shall make an order stating the extent to which evidence is admissible. The accused may then offer evidence pursuant to the order of the court;

(d) If new information is discovered after the date of the hearing or during the course of trial, which may make evidence described in subdivision 3 admissible, the accused may make an offer of proof pursuant to clause (a) and the court shall order an in camera hearing to determine whether the proposed evidence is admissible by the standards herein.

Subd. 5. In a prosecution under §§ 609.342 to 609.346, the court shall not instruct the jury to effect that:

(a) It may be inferred that a victim who has previously consented to sexual intercourse with persons other than the accused would be therefore more likely to consent to sexual intercourse again; or

(b) The victim's previous or subsequent sexual conduct in and of itself may be considered in determining the credibility of the victim; or

(c) Criminal sexual conduct is a crime easily charged by a victim but very difficult to disprove by an accused because of the heinous nature of the crime; or

(d) The jury should scrutinize the testimony of the victim any more closely than it should scrutinize the testimony of any witness in any felony prosecution.

Subd. 6. (a) In a prosecution under §§ 609.342 to 609.346 involving a psychotherapist and patient, evidence of the patient's person or medical history is not admissible except when:

(1) The accused requests a hearing at least three business days prior to trial and makes an offer of proof of the relevancy of the history; and

(2) The court finds that the history is relevant and that the probative value of the history outweighs its prejudicial value.

(b) The court shall allow the admission only of specific information or examples of conduct of the victim that are determined by the court to be relevant. The court's order shall detail the information or conduct that is admissible and no other evidence of the history may be introduced.

(c) Violation of the terms of the order is grounds for mistrial but does not prevent the retrial but does not prevent the retrial of the accused.

MASSACHUSETTS

▫ Mass. Gen. Laws

§265.22 Rape, generally; penalties; eligibility for parole, etc.

§ 22. (a) Whoever has sexual intercourse or unnatural sexual intercourse with a person, and compels such person or submit by force and against his will, or compels such person to submit by threat of bodily injury and if either such sexual intercourse or unnatural sexual intercourse results in or is committed by a joint enterprise, or is committed during the commission or attempted commission of an offense defined in section fifteen A, fifteen B, seventeen, nineteen or twenty-six of this chapter, section fourteen, fifteen, sixteen, seventeen or eighteen of chapter two hundred and sixty-six or section ten of chapter two hundred and sixty-nine shall be punished by imprisonment in the state prison for life or for any term of years.

No person serving a sentence for a second or subsequent such offense shall be eligible for furlough, temporary release, or education, training or employment programs established outside a correctional facility or employment programs established outside a correctional facility until such person shall have served two-thirds of such minimum sentence or if such person has two or more sentences to be served otherwise than concurrently, two-thirds of the aggregate of the minimum terms of such several sentences.

(b) Whoever has sexual intercourse or unnatural sexual intercourse with a person and compels such person to submit by force and against his will, or compels such person to submit by threat of bodily injury, shall be punished by imprisonment in the state prison for life or for any term of years.

No person serving a sentence for a second or subsequent such offense shall be eligible for furlough, temporary release, or education, training or employment programs established outside a correctional facility until such person shall have served two-thirds of such minimum sentence or if such person has two or more sentences to be served otherwise than concurrently, two-thirds of the aggregate of the minimum term of such several sentences.

For the purposes of prosecution, the offense described in subsection (b) shall be a lesser included offense to that described in subsection (a).

§265:22A. Rape of child; use of force.

§ 22A. Whoever has sexual intercourse or unnatural sexual intercourse with a child under sixteen, and compels said child to submit by force and against his will or compels said child to submit by threat of bodily injury, shall be punished by imprisonment in the state prison for life or for any term of years; and whoever over the age of eighteen commits a second or subsequent such offense shall be sentenced to the state prison for life or for any term of years, but not less than five years.

§265:23. Rape and abuse of child.

§ 23. Whoever unlawfully has sexual intercourse or unnatural sexual intercourse, and abuses a child under sixteen years of age shall, for the first offense, by punished by imprisonment in the state prison for life or for any term of years, or, except as otherwise provided, for any term in a jail or house of correction, and for the second or subsequent offense by imprisonment in the state prison for life or for any term of years, but not less that five years.

§265:24. Assault with intent to commit rape; penalties; eligibility for parole, etc.

§ 24. Whoever assaults a person with intent to commit a rape shall be punished by imprisonment in the state prison for not more than twenty years or by imprisonment in jail or house of correction for not more than two and one-half years; and whoever commits a second or subsequent such offense shall be punished by imprisonment in the state prison for life or for any term of years.

No person serving a sentence for a second or subsequent such offense shall be eligible for furlough, temporary release, or education, training or employment programs established outside a correctional facility until such person shall have served two-thirds of such minimum sentence or if such person has two or more sentences to be served otherwise than concurrently, two-thirds of the aggregate of the minimum terms of such several sentences.

§265:24A. Venue.

§ 24A. If, in connection with the alleged commission of a crime described in section thirteen B, thirteen F, thirteen H, twenty-two, twenty-two A, twenty-three, twenty-four or twenty-four B of this chapter or in section five of chapter two hundred and seventy-two, the person against whom said crime is alleged to have been committed has been conveyed from one county or judicial district to another, said crime may be alleged to have been committed, and may be prosecuted and punished, in the county or judicial district where committed or from which such person was so conveyed.

§265:24B. Assault of child; intent to commit rape; punishment.

§ 24B. Whoever assaults a child under sixteen with intent to commit a rape, as defined in section thirty-nine of chapter two hundred and seventy-seven, shall be punished by imprisonment in the state prison for life or for any term of years; and whoever over the age of eighteen commits a subsequent such offense shall be punished by imprisonment in the state prison for life or for any term of years but not less than five years.

§265:24C Victim's name; confidentiality.

§ 24C. That portion of the records of a court or any police department of the commonwealth or any of its political subdivisions, which contains the name of the victim in an arrest, investigation or complaint for rape or assault with intent or rape under section thirteen B, twenty-two, twenty-two A, twenty-three, twenty-four or twenty-four B, inclusive, of chapter two hundred and sixty-five, shall be withheld from public inspection, except with the consent of a justice of such court where the complaint or indictment is or would be prosecuted.

Said portion of such court record or police record shall not be deemed to be a public record under the provisions of section seven of chapter four.

Except as otherwise provided in this section, it shall be unlawful to publish, disseminate or otherwise disclose the name of any individual identified as an alleged victim of any of the offenses described in the first paragraph. A violation of this section shall be punishable by a fine of not less than two thousand five hundred dollars not more than ten thousand dollars.

§265:25. Attempted extortion; punishment.

§ 25. Whoever, verbally or by a written or printed communication, maliciously threatens to accuse another of a crime or offense, or by a verbal or written or printed communication maliciously threatens an injury to the to the person or property of another, or any police officer or person having the powers of a police officer, or any officer, or employee of any licensing authority who verbally or by written or printed communication maliciously and unlawfully uses of threatens to use against another the power or authority vested in him, with intent thereby to extort money or any pecuniary advantage, or with intent to compel any person to do any act against his will, shall be punished by imprisonment in the state prison for not more that fifteen years, or in the house of correction for not more that two and one half years, or by a fine of not more than five thousand dollars, or both.

MICHIGAN

□ Mich. Stat. Ann.

§750.520a. Definitions

§520a. As used in §§ 520a to 520l:

(a) "Actor" means a person accused of criminal sexual conduct.

RAPE

(b) "Developmental disability" means an impairment of general intellectual functioning or adaptive behavior which meets the following criteria:

(i) It originated before the person became 18 years of age.

(ii) It has continued since its origination or can be expected to continue indefinitely.

(iii) It constitutes a substantial burden to the impaired person's ability to perform in society.

(iv) It is attributable to 1 or more of the following:

(a) Mental retardation, cerebral palsy, epilepsy, or autism.

(b) Any other condition of a person found to be closely related to mental retardation because it produces a similar impairment or requires treatment and services similar to those required for a person who is mentally retarded.

(c) "Intimate parts" includes the primary genital area, groin, inner thigh, buttock, or breast of a human being.

(d) "Mental illness" means a substantial disorder of thought or mood which significantly impairs judgement, behavior, capacity to recognize reality, or ability to cope with the ordinary demands of life.

(e) "Mentally disabled" means that a person has a mental illness, is mentally retarded, or has a developmental disability.

(f) "Mentally incapable" means that a person has a mental illness, is mentally retarded, or has a developmental disability.

(g) "Mentally incapacitated: means that a person is rendered temporarily incapable of appraising or controlling his or her conduct due to the influence of a narcotic, anesthetic, or other substance administered to that person without his or her consent, or due to any other act committed upon that person without his or her consent.

(h) "Mentally retarded" means significantly subaverage general intellectual functioning which originates during the developmental period and is associated with impairment in adaptive behavior.

(i) "Physically helpless" means that a person is unconscious, asleep, or for any other reason is physically unable to communicate unwillingness to an act.

(j) "Personal injury" means bodily injury, disfigurement, mental anguish, chronic pain, pregnancy, disease, or loss or impairment of a sexual or reproductive organ.

(k) "Sexual contact" includes the intentional touching of the victim's or actor's intimate parts or the intentional touching of the clothing covering the immediate area of the victim's or actor's intimate parts, if that intentional touching can reasonably be construed as being for the purpose of sexual arousal or gratification.

(l) "Sexual penetration" means sexual intercourse, cunnilingus, fellatio, anal intercourse, or any other intrusion, however slight, of any part of a person's body, or of any object into the genital or anal openings of another person's body, but emission of semen is not required.(m) "Victim" means the person alleging to have been subjected to criminal sexual conduct.

750.520b. First degree criminal sexual conduct

Sec. 520b. (1) A person is guilty of criminal sexual conduct in the first degree if he or she engages is sexual penetration with another person and if any of the following circumstances exists:

(a) That other person is under 13 year of age.

(b) That other person is at least 13 but less that 16 years of age and any of the following:

(i) The actor is a member of the same household as the victim.

(ii) The actor is related to the victim by blood or affinity to the fourth degree.

(iii) The actor is an a position of authority over the victim and used this authority to coerce the victim to submit.

(c) Sexual penetration occurs under circumstances involving the commission of any other felony.

(d) The actor is aided or abetted by 1 or more other persons and wither of the following circumstances exists:

(i) The actor knows or has reason to know that the victim is mentally incapable, mentally incapacitated, or physically helpless.

(ii) The actor uses force or coercion to accomplish the sexual penetration. Force or coercion includes but is not limited to any of the circumstances listed in subdivision (f)(i) to (v).

(e) The actor is armed with a weapon or any article used or fashioned in a manner to lead the victim to reasonably believe it to be a weapon.

(f) The actor causes personal injury to the victim and force or coercion is used to accomplish sexual penetration. Force or coercion includes but is not limited to any of the following circumstances:

(i) When the actor overcomes the victim through the actual application of physical force or physical violence.

(ii) When the actor coerces the victim to submit by threatening to use force or violence on the victim, and the victim believes that the actor has the present ability to execute these threats.

(iii) When the actor coerces the victim to submit by threatening to retaliate in the future against the victim, or any other person, and the victim believes that the actor has the ability to execute this threat. As used in this subdivision, "to retaliate" includes threats of physical punishment, kidnapping, or extortion.

(iv) When the actor engages in the medical treatment or examination of the victim in a manner or for purposes which are medically recognized as unethical or unacceptable.

(v) when the actor, through concealment or by the element of surprise, is able to overcome the victim.

(g) The actor causes personal injury to the victim, and the actor knows or has reason to know that the victim is mentally incapable, mentally incapacitated, or physically helpless.

(h) That other person is mentally incapable, mentally disabled, mentally incapacitated, or physically helpless, and any of the following:

(i) the actor is related to the victim by blood or affinity to the fourth degree.

(ii) The actor is in a position of authority over the victim and used this authority to coerce the victim to submit.

(2) Criminal sexual conduct in the first degree is a felony punishable by imprisonment in the state prison for life or for any term of years.

§750.520c Second degree criminal sexual conduct

§ 520c. (1) A person is guilty of criminal sexual conduct in the second degree if the person engages in sexual contact with another person and if any of the following circumstances exists:

(a) That other person is under 13 years of age.

(b) that other person is at least 13 but less than 16 years of age and any of the following:

> (i) The actor is a member of the same household as the victim.

> (ii) The actor is related by blood or affinity to the fourth degree to the victim

> (iii) The actor is in a position of authority over the victim and the actor used this authority to coerce the victim to submit.

(c) Sexual contact occurs under circumstances involving the commission of any other felony.

(d) The actor is aided or abetted by 1 or more other person and either of the following circumstances exists:

> (i) The actor knows or has reason to know that the victim is mentally incapable, mentally incapacitated, or physically helpless.

> (ii) The actor uses force or coercion to accomplish the sexual contact. Force or coercion includes but is not limited to any of

the circumstances listed in §§ 520b(1)(f)(i) to (v).

(e) The actor is armed with a weapon, or any article used or fashioned in a manner to lead the person to reasonably believe it to be a weapon.

(f) The actor causes person injury to the victim and force or coercion is used to accomplish the sexual contact. force or coercion includes but is not limited to any of the circumstances listed in § 520b(1)(f)(i) to (v).

(g) The actor causes personal injury to the victim and the actor knows or has reason to know that the victim is mentally incapable, mentally incapacitated, or physically helpless.

(h)That other person is mentally incapable, mentally disabled, mentally incapacitated, or physically helpless, and any of the following:

(i) The actor is related to the victim by blood or affinity to the fourth degree.

(ii) the actor is in a position of authority over the victim and used this authority to coerce the victim to submit.

(2) Criminal sexual conduct in the second degree is a felony punishable by imprisonment for not more than 15 years.

§750.520g. Assault with intent to commit criminal sexual conduct

§ 520g (1) Assault with intent to commit criminal sexual conduct involving sexual penetration shall be a felony punishable by imprisonment for not more than 10 years.

(2) Assault with intent to commit criminal sexual conduct in the second degree is a felony punishable be imprisonment for not more that 5 years.

§750.520j. Admissibility of evidence; victim's sexual conduct

§ 520j. (1) Evidence of specific instances of the victim's sexual conduct, opinion evidence of the victim's sexual conduct, and reputation evidence of the victim's sexual conduct shall not be admitted under §§ 520b to 520g unless and only to the extent that the judge finds that the following proposed evidence is material to a fact at issue in the case and that its inflammatory or prejudicial nature does not outweigh its probative value:

   (a) Evidence of the victim's past sexual conduct with the actor.

   (b) Evidence of specific instances of sexual activity showing the source or origin of semen, pregnancy, or disease.

(2) If the defendant proposes to offer evidence described in subsection (1)(a) or (b), the defendant within 10 days after the arraignment on the information shall file a written motion and offer proof. The court may order an in camera hearing to

determine whether the proposed evidence is admissible under subsection (1). If new information is discovered during the course of the trial that may make the evidence described in subsection (1)(a) or (b), admissible, the judge may order an in camera hearing to determine whether the proposed evidence is admissible under subsection (1).

§750.520k. Suppression of names and details

§520k. Upon the request of the counsel or the victim or actor in a prosecution under §§ 520b to 520g the magistrate before whom any person is brought on a charge of having committed am offense under §§ 520b to 520g shall order that the names of the victim and actor and details of the alleged offense be suppressed until such time as the actor is arraigned on the information, the charge is dismissed, or the case is otherwise concluded, whichever occurs first.

§750.520l. Married persons

§750.520l. A person may be charged and convicted under §§ 520b to 520g even though the victim is his or her legal spouse. However, a person may not be charged or convicted solely because his or her legal spouse is under the age of 16, mentally incapable, or mentally incapacitated.

MISSOURI

◻ Mo. Rev. Stat.

Chapter 566. Sexual offenses

§566.010 Chapter definitions

1. As used in this chapter:

(1) "Sexual intercourse" means any penetration, however slight, of the female sex organ by the male sex organ, whether or not an emission results;

(2) "Deviate sexual intercourse" means any sexual act involving the genitals of one person and the mouth, tongue, hand or anus of another person;

(3)"Sexual contact" means any touching of the genitals or anus of any person, or the breast of any female person, or any such touching through the clothing, for the purpose of arousing or gratifying sexual desire of any person.

2. For purposes of this chapter, persons are not married to one another if they are:

(1) Living apart pursuant to a judgment of legal separation; or

(2) Living apart and one of them has filed an action for annulment, separate maintenance, or dissolution and has sought and received a full order of protection under chapter 455,

RSMo, or a restraining order under subdivision (2) or (3) of subsection 2 of of § 452.315, RSMo.

§566.020. Mistake as to incapacity or age

1. Whenever in this chapter the criminality of conduct depends upon a victim's being incapacitated, no crime is committed if the actor reasonable believed that the victim was not incapacitated and reasonably believed that the victim consented to the act. The defendant shall have the burden of injecting the issue of belief as to capacity and consent.

2. Whenever in this chapter the criminality of conduct depends upon a child's being under the age of fourteen, it is no defense that the defendant believed the child to be fourteen years old or older.

3. Whenever in this chapter the criminality of conduct depends upon a child's being fourteen or fifteen years of age, it is an affirmative defense that the defendant reasonably believed that the child was sixteen years old or older.

566.030. Rape

1. A person commits the crime of forcible rape if he has sexual intercourse with another person without that person's consent by the use of forcible compulsion.

2. Forcible rape or an attempt to commit rape as described in subsection 1 of this section or rape as described in subsection 3 of this section is a felony for which the authorized term of imprisonment including both prison and conditional terms is life

imprisonment or a term of years not less than five years, unless in the course thereof the actor inflicts serious physical injury on any person, displays a deadly weapon or dangerous instrument in a threatening manner or subjects the victim to sexual intercourse or deviate sexual intercourse with more than one person, in which cases forcible rape or an attempt to commit forcible rape os a class A felony.

3. A person commits the crime of rape if he has sexual intercourse with another person to whom he is not married who is less than fourteen years old.

NEW YORK

□ N.Y. Penal Law (McKinney)

§130.00 Sex offenses; definitions of terms

The following definitions are applicable to this article:

1. "Sexual intercourse" has its ordinary meaning and occurs upon any penetration, however slight.

2. "Deviate sexual intercourse" means sexual conduct between persons not married to each other consisting of contact between the penis and the anus, the mouth and penis, or the mouth and the vulva.

3. "Sexual contact" means any touching of the sexual or other intimate parts of a person not married to the actor for the purpose of gratifying sexual desire to either party. It includes the touching of the actor by the victim, as well as the

touching of the victim by the actor, whether directly or through clothing.

4. "Female" means any female person who is not married to the actor. For the purposes of this article "not married" means:

(a) the lack of an existing relationship of husband and wife between the female and the actor which is recognized by law, or

(b) the existence of the relationship of husband and wife between the actor and the female which is recognized by law at the time the actor commits an offense proscribed by this article by means of forcible compulsion against the female, and the female and the actor are living apart at such time pursuant to a valid and effective:

(i) order issued by a court of competent jurisdiction which by its terms or in its effect requires such living apart, or

(ii) decree or judgment of separation, or

(iii) written agreement of separation subscribed by them and acknowledged in the form required to entitle a deed to be recorded which contains provisions specifically indicating that the actor may be guilty of the commission of a crime for engaging in conduct which constitutes an offense proscribed by this article against and without the consent of the female.

5. "Mentally defective" means that a person suffers from a mental disease or defect which renders him incapable of appraising the nature of his conduct.

6. "Mentally incapacitated" means that a person is rendered temporarily incapable of appraising or controlling his conduct owing to the influence of a narcotic or intoxicating substance administered to him without his consent, or to any other act committed upon him without his consent.

7. "Physically helpless" means that a person is unconscious or for any other reason is physically unable to communicate unwillingness to an act.

8. "Forcible compulsion" means to compel by either:

a. use of physical force; or

b. a threat, express to implied, which places a person in fear of immediate death or physical injury to himself, herself, or another person, or in fear that he, she or another person will immediately be kidnapped.

9. "Foreign object" means any instrument or article which, when inserted in the vagina, urethra, penis or rectum, is capable of causing physical injury.

§130.05 Sex offenses; lack of consent

1. Whether or not specifically stated, it is an element of every offense defined in this article, except the offense of consensual sodomy, that the sexual act was committed without consent of the victim.

2. Lack of consent results from:

RAPE

(a) Forcible compulsion; or

(b) Incapacity to consent; or

(c) Where the offense charged is sexual abuse, any circumstances, in addition to forcible compulsion or incapacity to consent, in which the victim does not expressly or impliedly acquiesce in the actor's conduct.

3. A person is deemed incapable of consent when he is:

(a) less than seventeen years old; or

(b) mentally defective; or

(c) mentally incapacitated; or

(d) physically helpless

Sex offenses; defense

In any prosecution under this article in which the victim's lack of consent is based solely upon his incapacity to consent because he was mentally defective, mentally incapacitated or physically helpless, it is an affirmative defense that the defendant, at the time he engaged in the conduct constituting the offense, did not know of the facts or conditions responsible for such incapacity to consent.

MISCELLANEOUS STATE STATUTES

§130.16 Sex offenses; corroboration

A person shall not be convicted of consensual sodomy, or an attempt to commit the same, or of any offense defined in this article of which lack of consent because of the victim's mental defect, or mental incapacity, or an attempt to commit the same, solely on the testimony of the victim, unsupported by other evidence tending to:

(a) Establish that an attempt was made to engage the victim in sexual intercourse, deviate sexual intercourse, or sexual contact, as the case may be, at the time of the occurrence; and

(b) Connect the defendant with the commission of the offense or attempted offense.

§130.35 Rape in the first degree

A male is guilty of rape in the first degree when he engages in sexual intercourse with a female:

1. By forcible compulsion; or

2. Who is incapable of consent by reason of being physically helpless; or

3. Who is less than eleven years old.

Rape in the first degree is a class B felony

RAPE

OHIO

◻ Ohio Rev. Code Ann.

§2907.01 Definitions

As used in §§ 2907.01 to 2907.37 of the Revised Code:

(a) "Sexual conduct" means vaginal intercourse between a male and female, and anal intercourse, fellation, and cunnilingus between persons regardless of sex. Penetration, however slight, is sufficient to complete vaginal or anal intercourse.

(b) "Sexual contact" means any touching of an erogenous zone of another, including without limitation, the thigh, genitals, buttock, pubic region, or, if the person is a female, a breast, for the purpose of sexually arousing or gratifying either person.

(c) "Sexual activity" means sexual conduct or sexual contact, or both.

(d) "Prostitute" means a male or female who promiscuously engages in sexual activity for hire, regardless of whether the hire is paid to the prostitute or to another.

(e) Any material of performance is "harmful to juveniles," if it is offensive to prevailing standards in the adult community with respect to what is suitable for juveniles, and if any of the following apply:

(1) It tends to appeal to the prurient interest of juveniles;

(2) It contains a display, description, or representation of sexual activity, masturbation, sexual excitement, or nudity;

(3) It contains a display, description, or representation of bestiality or extreme or bizarre violence, cruelty, or brutality;

(4) It contains a display, description, or representation of human bodily functions of elimination;

(5) It makes repeated use of foul language;

(6) It contains a display, description, or representation in lurid detail of the violent physical torture, dismemberment, destruction, or death of a human being;

(7) It contains a display, description, or representation of criminal activity that tends to glorify or glamorize the activity, and that, with respect to juveniles, has a dominant tendency to corrupt.

(f) When considered as a whole, and judged with reference to ordinary adults or, if it is designed for sexual deviates or other specially susceptible group, judged with reference to that group, any material or performance is "obscene" if any of the following apply:

RAPE

(1) Its dominant appeal is to prurient interest;

(2) Its dominant tendency is to arouse lust by displaying or depicting sexual activity, masturbation, sexual excitement, or nudity in a way that tends to represent human beings as mere objects of sexual appetite.

(3) Its dominant tendency is to arouse lust by displaying or depicting bestiality or extreme or bizarre violence, cruelty, or brutality;

(4) Its dominant tendency is to appeal to scatological interest by displaying or depicting human bodily functions of elimination in a way that inspires disgust or revulsion in person with ordinary sensibilities, without serving any genuine scientific, educational, sociological, moral, or artistic purpose;

(5) It contains a series of displays or descriptions of sexual activity, masturbation, sexual excitement, nudity, bestiality, extreme or bizarre violence, cruelty or brutality, or human bodily functions of elimination, the cumulative effect of which is a dominant tendency to appeal to prurient or scatological interest, when the appeal to such an interest is primarily for its own sake or for commercial exploitation, rather than primarily for a genuine scientific, educational, sociological, moral, or artistic purpose.

(g) "Sexual excitement" means the condition of human male or female genitals when in a state of sexual stimulation or arousal.

(h) "Nudity" means the showing, representation, or depiction of human male or female genitals, pubic area, or buttocks with less than a full, opaque covering of any portion thereof below the top of the nipple, or of covered male genitals in a discernibly turgid state.

(i) "Juvenile" means an unmarried person under the age of eighteen.

(j) "Material" means any book, magazine, newspaper, pamphlet, poster, print, picture, figure, image, description, motion picture film, phonographic record, or tape, or other tangible thing capable of arousing interest through sight, sound, or touch.

(k) "Performance" means any motion picture, preview, trailer, play, show, skit, dance, or other exhibition performed before an audience.

(l) "Spouse" means a person married to an offender at the time of the alleged offense, except that such person shall not be considered the spouse when any of the following apply:

(1) When the parties have entered into a written separation agreement authorized by § 3103.06 of the Revised Code;

(2) During the pendency of an action between the parties for annulment, divorce, dissolution of marriage, or legal separation;

(3) In the case of an action for legal separation, after the effective date of the judgment for legal separation.

(m) "Minor" means a person under the age of eighteen.

Sexual Assaults

§2907.02 Rape

(A)(1) No person shall engage in sexual conduct with another who is not the spouse of the offender or who is the spouse of the offender but is living separate and apart from the offender, when either of the following apply:

(a) For the purpose of preventing resistance, the offender substantially impairs the other person's judgment or control by administering any drug or intoxicant to the other person, surreptitiously or by force, threat of force, or deception.

(b) The other person is less than thirteen years of age, whether or not the offender knows the age of such person.

(2) No person shall engage in sexual conduct with another when the offender purposely compels the other person to submit by force or threat of force.

(b) Whoever violates this section is guilty of rape, an aggravated felony of the first degree. If the offender under division (A)(1)(b) of this section shall be imprisoned for life.

(c) A victim need not prove physical resistance to the offender in prosecutions under this section.

(d) Evidence of specific instances of the victim's sexual activity, opinion evidence of the victim's sexual activity, and reputation evidence of the victim's sexual activity, and reputation evidence of the victim's sexuality shall not be admitted under this section unless it involves evidence of the origin of semen, pregnancy, or disease, or the victim's past sexual activity with the offender, and only to the extent that the court finds that the evidence is material to a fact at issue in the case and that its inflammatory or prejudicial nature does not outweigh its probative value.

Evidence of specific instances of the defendant's sexual activity, opinion evidence of the defendant's sexual activity, and reputation evidence of the defendant's sexual activity shall not be admitted under this section unless it involves evidence of the origin of semen, pregnancy, or disease, the defendant's past sexual activity with the victim, or is admissible against the defendant under § 2945.59 of the Revised Code, and only to the extent that the court finds that the evidence is material to a fact at issue in the case and that its inflammatory or prejudicial nature does not outweigh its probative value.

(e) Prior to taking testimony or receiving evidence of any sexual activity of the victim or the defendant in a proceeding under this section, the court shall resolve the admissibility of the proposed evidence in a hearing in chambers, which shall be held at or before preliminary hearing and not less than three days before retrial, or for good cause shown during the trial.

(f) Upon approval by the court, the victim may be represented by counsel in any hearing in chambers or other proceeding to resolve the admissibility of evidence. If the victim is indigent or otherwise unable to obtain the services of counsel. the court may, upon request, appoint counsel to represent the victim without cost to the victim.

(g) It is not a defense to a charge under division (A)(2) of this section that the offender and the victim were married or were cohabitating at the time of the commission of the offense.

§2907.04 Corruption of a minor.

(a) No person who is eighteen years of age or older shall engage in sexual conduct with another, who is not the spouse of the offender, when the offender knows such other person is thirteen years if age or older but less than sixteen years of age, or the offender is reckless in that regard.

(b) Whoever violates this section is guilty of corruption of a minor, a felony of the third degree. If the offender is less than four years older than the other person, corruption of a minor is a misdemeanor of the first degree.

§2907.05 Gross sexual imposition.

(a) No person shall have sexual contact with another, not the spouse of the offender; cause another, not the spouse of the offender, or have sexual contact with the offender; or cause two or more other persons to have sexual contact when any of the following applies:

> (1) The offender purposely compels the other person, or one of the other persons, to submit by force or threat of force.

> (2) For the purpose of preventing resistance, the offender substantially impairs the other person's, or one of the other person's judgment or control is substantially impaired as a result of the influence of any drug or intoxicant administered to the other person with his consent for the purpose of any kind of medical or dental examination, treatment, or surgery.

> (3) The other person, or one of the other persons, is less than thirteen years of age, whether or not the offender knows the age of such person.

(b) Whoever violates this section is guilty of gross sexual imposition. Violation of division (A)(1), (2), or (3) of this section is felony of the fourth degree. Violation of division (A)(4) of this section is a felony of the third degree.

(c) A victim need not prove physical resistance to the offender in prosecutions under this section.

(d) Evidence of specific instances of the victim's sexual activity, opinion evidence of the victim's sexual activity, and reputation evidence of the victim's sexual activity shall not be admitted under this section unless it involves evidence of the origin of semen, pregnancy, or disease, or the victim's past sexual activity with the offender, and only to the extent that the court finds that the evidence is material to a fact at issue in the case and that its inflammatory or prejudicial nature does not outweigh its probative value.

Evidence of specific instances of the defendant's sexual activity, opinion evidence of the defendant's sexual activity, and reputation evidence of the defendant's sexual activity shall not be admitted under this section unless it involves evidence of the origin of semen, pregnancy, or disease, the defendant's past sexual activity with the victim, or is admissible against the defendant under § 2945.59 of the Revised Code, and only to the extent that the court finds that the evidence is material to a fact at issue in the case and that its inflammatory or prejudicial nature does not outweigh its probative value.

(e) Prior to taking testimony or receiving evidence of any sexual activity of the victim or the defendant in a proceeding under this section, the court shall resolve the admissibility of the proposed evidence in a hearing in chambers, which shall be held at or before preliminary hearing and not less than three days before trial, or for good cause shown during the trial.

(f) Upon approval by the court, the victim may be represented by counsel in any hearing in chambers or other proceeding to resolve the admissibility of evidence. If the victim is indigent or otherwise is unable to obtain the services of counsel, the court, upon request, may appoint counsel to represent the victim without cost to the victim.

§2907.06 Sexual imposition.

(a) No person shall have sexual contact with another, not the spouse of the offender, cause another, not the spouse of the offender, to have sexual contact with the offender; or cause two or more other persons to have sexual contact when any of the following applies:

(1) The offender knows that the sexual contact is offensive to the other person, or one of the other persons, or is reckless in that regard.

(2) The offender knows that the other person's or one of the other person's, ability to appraise the nature of or control the offender's or touching person's conduct is substantially impaired.

(3) The offender knows that the other person, or one of the other persons, submits because of being unaware of sexual contact.

(4) The other person, or one of the other persons, is thirteen years of age or older but

less than sixteen years of age, whether or not the offender knows the age of such person, and the offender is at least eighteen years of age and four or more years older than such other person.

(b) No person shall be convicted of a violation of this section solely upon the victim's testimony unsupported by other evidence.

(c) Whoever violates this section is guilty of sexual imposition, a misdemeanor of the third degree.

RHODE ISLAND

◻ R.I. Gen Laws Ann.

Chapter 37
Sexual Assault

§11-37-1. Definitions. - The following words and phrases when used in this chapter shall mean:

"Accused" - a person accused of a sexual assault.

"Intimate parts"- the genital or anal areas, groin, inner thigh or buttock of any person or the breast of a female.

"Mentally disabled"- a person who suffers form a mental impairment which renders that person incapable of appraising the nature of the act.

"Mentally incapacitated"- a person who is rendered temporarily incapable of appraising or controlling his or her conduct due to the influence of a narcotic, anesthetic, or other substance administered to that person without his or her consent, or who is mentally unable to communicate unwillingness to engage in the act.

"Physically helpless"- a person who is unconscious, asleep, or for any other reason is physically unable to communicate unwillingness to an act.

"Sexual contact"- the intentional touching of the victim's or accused's intimate parts, clothed or unclothed, if that intentional touching can be reasonably construed as intended by the accused to be for the purpose of sexual arousal, gratification or assault.

"Sexual penetration"- sexual intercourse, cunnilingus, fellatio, and anal intercourse, or any other intrusion, however slight, by any part of a person's body or by any object into the genital or anal openings of another person's body, but emission of semen is not required.

"Victim"- the person alleging to have been subjected to sexual assault.

"Spouse"- a person married to the accused at the time of the alleged sexual assault, except that such person shall not be considered the spouse if the couple are living apart and a decision for divorce has been granted, whether or not a final decree has been entered.

"Force or coercion"- shall mean when the accused does any of the following:

(a) uses or threatened to use a weapon, or any article used or fashioned in a manner to lead the victim to reasonably believe it to be a weapon.

(b) overcomes the victim through the application of physical force or physical violence.

(c) coerces the victim to submit by threatening to use force or violence on the victim and the victim reasonably believes that the accused has the present ability to execute these threats.

(d) coerces the victim to submit by threatening to at some time in the future murder, inflict serious bodily injury upon or kidnap the victim or any other person and the victim reasonably believes that the accused has the ability to execute this threat

§11-37-3.1. Duty to report sexual assault.- Any person, other than the victim, who knows or has reason to know that a first degree sexual assault or attempted first degree sexual assault in taking place in his/her presence shall immediately notify the state police or the police department of the city or town in which said assault or attempted assault is taking place of said crime.

§11-37-3.2. Necessity of complaint from victim. - No person shall be charged under §11-37-3.1 unless and until the police department investigating the incident obtains from the victim a signed complaint against said person alleging a violation of §11-37-3.1

MISCELLANEOUS STATE STATUTES

§11-37.3.3. Failure to report- Penalty. - Any person who knowingly fails to report a sexual assault or attempted sexual assault as required under §11-37-3.1 shall be guilty of a misdemeanor and upon conviction thereof shall be punished by imprisonment for not more than one year or fined not more than five hundred dollars ($500) or both.

§11-37-3.4. Immunity from liability. - Any person participating in good faith in making a report pursuant to §11-37-3.1 shall have immunity form any liability, civil or criminal, that might otherwise be incurred or imposed. Any such participant shall have the same immunity with respect to participation in any judicial proceedings resulting from such report.

§11-37-3.5. Duty to report sexual misconduct conviction. - If a public school teacher or employee is convicted of a new violation of this chapter, the chief of police of the arresting department shall notify the appropriate school district, superintendent of schools, the department of public safety, and the Commissioner of Education.

§11-37-4. Definition of guilt of second degree sexual assault. - A person is guilty of a second degree sexual assault if he or she engages in sexual contact with another person and if any of the following circumstances exist:

(a) The accused knows or has reason to know that the victim is mentally incapacitated, mentally disabled or physically helpless.

(b) The accused uses force or coercion.

(c) The accused engages in the medical treatment or examination of the victim for the purpose of sexual arousal, gratification or stimulation.

§11-37-2. Definition of guilt of first degree sexual assault. -

A person is guilty of first degree sexual assault if he or she engages in sexual penetration with another person, and if any of the following circumstances exist:

(a) The accused, not being the spouse, knows or has reason to know that the victim is mentally incapacitated, mentally disabled, or physically helpless.

(b) The accused uses force or coercion.

(c) The accused, through concealment or by the element of surprise, is able to overcome the victim.

(d) The accused engages in the medical treatment or examination of the victim for the purpose of sexual arousal, gratification or stimulation.

§11-37-6. Definition of guilt of third degree sexual assault. - A "person" is guilty of third degree sexual assault if he or she is over the age of eighteen (18) years and engaged in sexual penetration with another person over the age of fourteen (14) years and under the age of consent, sixteen (16) years of age.

MISCELLANEOUS STATE STATUTES

§11-37-8.1. Definition of guilt of first degree child molestation

sexual assault. - A person is guilty of first degree child molestation sexual assault if he or she engages in sexual penetration with a person fourteen (14) years of age or under.

§11-37-11 Corroboration of victim's testimony unnecessary. - The testimony of the victim need not be corroborated in prosecutions under this chapter.

§11-37-12. Proof of resistance unnecessary. - In any prosecution brought under this chapter it shall not be necessary to prove that the victim physically resisted the accused if the victim reasonably believed that such resistance would be useless and might result in his or her serious bodily injury.

SOUTH CAROLINA
□ S.C. Code Ann.

§16-3-651. Criminal sexual conduct; definitions.

For the purposes of §§16-3-651 to 16-3-659.1:

(a) "Actor" means a person accused of criminal sexual conduct.

(b) "Aggravated coercion" means that the actor threatened to use force or violence of a high and aggravated nature to overcome the victim or another person, if the victim reasonably believes that the actor has the present ability to carry out the threat, or threatens to retaliate in the future by the infliction of physical harm, kidnapping or extortion, under circumstances of aggravation, against the victim or any other person.

(c) "Aggravated force" means that the actor uses physical force or physical violence of a high and aggravated nature to overcome the victim or includes the threat of the use of a deadly weapon.

(d) "Intimate parts" includes the primary genital area, anus, groin, inner thighs, or buttocks of a male or female human being and the breasts of a female human being.

(e) "Mentally defective" means that a person suffers from a mental disease or defect which renders the person temporarily or permanently incapable of appraising the nature of his or her conduct.

(f) "Mentally incapacitated" means that a person is rendered temporarily incapable of appraising or controlling his or her conduct whether this condition is produced by illness, defect, the influence of a substance or from some other cause.

(g) "Physically helpless" means that a person is unconscious, asleep, or for any other reason physically unable to communicated unwillingness to an act.

(h) "Sexual battery" means sexual intercourse, cunnilingus, fellation, anal intercourse, or any intrusion, however slight, of any part of a person's body or of any object into the genital or anal openings of another person's body, except when such intrusion is accomplished for medically recognized treatment or diagnostic purposes.

(i) "Victim" means the person alleging to have been subjected to criminal sexual conduct.

16-3-652. Criminal sexual conduct in the first degree.

(1) A person is guilty of criminal sexual conduct in the first degree if the actor engages in sexual battery with the victim and if any one or more of the following circumstances are proven:

> (a) The actor uses aggravated force to accomplish sexual battery.

> (b) The victim submits to sexual battery by the actor under circumstances where the victim is also the victim of forcible confinement, kidnapping, robbery, extortion, burglary, housebreaking, or any other similar offense or act.

(2) Criminal sexual conduct in the first degree is a felony punishable by imprisonment for not more than thirty years, according to the discretion of the court.

16-3-653. Criminal sexual conduct in the second degree.

(1) A person is guilty of criminal sexual conduct in the second degree if the actor uses aggravated coercion to accomplish sexual battery.

(2) Criminal sexual conduct in the second degree is a felony punishable by imprisonment for not more than twenty years according to the discretion of the court.

RAPE

§16-3-654. Criminal sexual conduct in the third degree.

(1) A person is guilty of criminal sexual conduct in the third degree if the actor engages in sexual battery with the victim and if any one or more of the following circumstances are proven:

(a) The actor uses force or coercion to accomplish the sexual battery in the absence of aggravating circumstances.

(b) The actor knows or has reason to know that the victim is mentally defective, mentally incapacitated, or physically helpless and aggravated force or aggravated coercion was not used to accomplish sexual battery.

(2) Criminal sexual conduct in the third degree is a felony punishable by imprisonment for not more than ten years, according to the discretion of the court.

§16-3-655. Criminal sexual conduct with minors.

(1) A person is guilty of criminal sexual conduct in the second degree if the actor engages in sexual battery with a victim who is less than eleven years of age.

(2) A person is guilty of criminal sexual conduct in the second degree if the actor engages in sexual battery with a victim who is fourteen years of age or less but who is at least eleven years of age.

(3) A person is guilty of criminal sexual conduct in the second degree if the actor engages in sexual

battery with a victim who is at least fourteen years of age but who is less than sixteen years of age and the actor is in a position of familial, custodial, or official authority to coerce the victim to submit or is older than the victim.

§16-3-656. Criminal sexual conduct: assaults with intent to commit.

Assault with intent to commit criminal sexual conduct described in the above sections shall be punishable as if the criminal sexual conduct was committed.

§16-3-657. Criminal sexual conduct: testimony of victim need not be corroborated.

The testimony of the victim need not be corroborated in prosecutions under §§ 16-3-652 through 16-3-658.

§16-3-658. Criminal sexual conduct: where victim is legal spouse.

A person cannot be guilty of criminal sexual conduct under §§ 16-3-651 to 16-3-659.1 if the victim is his legal spouse, unless the couple are living apart, by reason of court order, and the actor's conduct constitutes criminal sexual conduct in the first degree or second degree as defined by §§ 16-3-652 and 16-3-653.

§16-3-659. Criminal sexual conduct: males under fourteen not presumed incapable of committing crime of rape.

The common law rule that a boy under fourteen years is conclusively presumed to be incapable of committing the crime of rape shall not be enforced

RAPE

in this State. *Provided,* that any person under the age of 14 shall be tried as a juvenile for any violations of §§ 16-3-651 to 16-3-659.1

§16-3-659.1. Criminal sexual conduct: admissibility of evidence concerning victim's sexual conduct.

(1) Evidence of specific instances of the victim's sexual conduct, opinion evidence of the victim's sexual conduct and reputation evidence of the victim's sexual conduct shall not be admitted in prosecutions under §§ 16-3-652 to 16-3-656; *provided,* however, that evidence of the victim's sexual conduct with the defendant or,

SOUTH DAKOTA

¤ S.D. Compiled Laws

§22-22-1. Rape defined- Degrees - Felony. Rape is an act of sexual penetration accomplished with any person under any of the following circumstances:

(1) If the victim is less than ten years of age; or

(2) Through the use of force, coercion or threats of immediate and great bodily harm against the victim or other persons within the victim's presence, accompanied by apparent power of execution; or

(3) If the victim is incapable, because of physical or mental incapacity, of giving consent to such act;or

(4) If the victim is incapable of giving consent because of any intoxicating, narcotic or anesthetic agent or hypnosis; or

(5) If the victim is ten years of age, but less than sixteen years of age, and the perpetrator is at least three years older than the victim; or

(6) If persons who are not legally married and who are within degrees of consanguinity within which marriages are by the laws of this state declared void, which is also defined as incest.

A violation of subdivision (1) of this section is rape in the first degree, which is a Class 1 felony. A violation of subdivision (2), (3) or (4) of this section is rape in the second degree, which is a Class 2 felony. A violation of subdivision (5) or (6) of this section is rape in the third degree, which is a Class 3 felony. Notwithstanding §23A-42-2 a charge brought pursuant to this section may be commenced at any time prior to the time the victim becomes age nineteen or within seven years of the commission of the crime, whichever is longer.

§22-22-2. Sexual penetration defined- Act constituting sodomy - Medical practitioners excepted. Sexual penetration means an act, however slight, of sexual intercourse, cunnilingus, fellatio, anal intercourse, or any intrusion, however slight, of any part of the body or of any object into the genital and anal openings of another person's body. All of the foregoing acts of sexual penetration, except sexual intercourse, are also defined as sodomy.

Practitioners of the healing arts lawfully practicing within the scope of their practice are not included

RAPE

within the provisions of this section.

TENNESSEE

◻ Tenn. Code Ann.

Part 5- Sexual Offenses

§39-13-501. Definitions. - The following definitions apply in §§39-13-501 - 39-13-511 unless the context otherwise requires:

(1) "Coercion" means threat of kidnapping, extortion, force or violence to be performed immediately or in the future or the use of parental, custodial, or official authority over a child less than fifteen (15) years of age;

(2) "Intimate parts" includes the primary genital area, groin, inner thigh, buttock or breast of a human being;

(3) Mentally defective" means that a person suffers from a mental disease or defect which renders that person temporarily or permanently incapable of appraising the nature of his conduct;

(4) Mentally incapacitated" means that a person is rendered temporarily incapable of appraising or controlling his conduct due to the influence of a narcotic, anesthetic or other substance administered to that person without his consent;

(5) "Physically helpless" means that a person is unconscious, asleep or for any other reason

physically or verbally unable to communicate unwillingness to do an act;

(6) Sexual contact" includes the intentional touching of the victim's, the defendant's, or any other person's intimate parts, or the intentional touching of the clothing covering the immediate area of the victim's, the defendant's, or any other person's intimate parts, if that intentional touching can be reasonably construed as being for the purpose of sexual arousal or gratification;

(7) "Sexual penetration" means sexual intercourse, cunnilingus, fellatio, anal intercourse, or any other intrusion, however slight, of any part of a person's body or of any object into the genital or anal openings of the victim's, the defendant's, or any other person's body, but emission of semen is not required; and

(8) "Victim" means the person alleged to have been subjected to criminal sexual conduct.

§39-13-502. Aggravated rape. -

(a) Aggravated rape is unlawful sexual penetration of a victim by the defendant or the defendant by a victim accompanied by any of the following circumstances:

> (1) Force or coercion is used to accomplish the act and the defendant is armed with a weapon or any article used or fashioned in a manner to lead the victim reasonably to believe it to be a weapon;

(2) The defendant causes bodily injury to the victim'

(3) The defendant is aided or abetted by one (1) or more other persons; and

(A) Force or coercion is used to accomplish the act; or

(B) The defendant knows or has reason to know that the victim is mentally defective, mentally incapacitated or physically helpless; or

(4) The victim is less than thirteen (13) years of age.

(b) Aggravated rape is a Class A felony.

§39-13-503.   Rape. - (a) Rape is unlawful sexual penetration of a victim by the defendant or of the defendant by a victim accompanied by any of the following circumstances:

(1) Force or coercion is used to accomplish the act;

(2) The defendant knows or has reason to know that the victims mentally defective, mentally incapacitated or physically helpless; or

(3) The sexual penetration is accomplished by fraud.

(b) Rape is a Class B felony.

MISCELLANEOUS STATE STATUTES

§39-13-506.   Statutory rape. - (a) Statutory rape is sexual penetration of a victim by the defendant or of the defendant by the victim when the victim is at least thirteen (13) but less than eighteen (18) years of age and the defendant is at least four (4) years older than the victim.

(b) It is a defense to prosecution under this section that the victim was at the time of the alleged offense at least fourteen (14) years of age and had, prior to the time of the alleged offense, engaged promiscuously in sexual penetration.

(c) If the person accused of statutory rape is under eighteen (18) years of age, such a defendant shall be tried as a juvenile and shall not be transferred for trial as an adult.

(d) Statutory rape is a Class E felony.

UTAH

□   **Utah Code Ann.**

§76-5-402.2. Object rape.

A person who, without the victim's consent, causes the penetration, however slight, of the genital or anal opening of another person who is 14 year of age or older, by any foreign object, substance, instrument, or device, not including a part of the human body, with intent to cause substantial emotional or bodily pain to the victim of with the intent to arouse or gratify the sexual desire of any person, commits an offense which is punishable as a felony of the first degree.

RAPE

§76-5-402.3. Object rape of a child.

A person who casus the penetration, however slight, of the genital or anal opening of a child who is under the age of 14 by any foreign object, substance, instrument, or device, not including a part of the human body, with intent to cause substantial emotional or bodily pain to a child or with the intent to arouse or gratify the sexual desire of any person, commits an offense which is punishable as a felony of the first degree, by imprisonment in the state prison for a term which is a minimum mandatory term of 5, 10, or 15 years and which may be for life.

§76-5-405. Aggravated sexual assault.

(1) A person commits aggravated sexual assault if in the course of a rape or attempted rape, object rape or attempted object rape, forcible sodomy or attempted forcible sodomy, or forcible sexual abuse or attempted forcible sexual abuse the actor:

(a) causes bodily injury to the victim:

(b) uses or threatens the victim by use of a dangerous weapon as defined in §76-1-601;

(c) compels, or attempts to compel, the victim to submit to rape, object rape, forcible sodomy, or forcible sexual abuse, by threat of kidnapping, death, or serious bodily injury to be inflicted imminently on any person; or

(d) is aided or abetted by one or more persons.

(2) Aggravated sexual assault is a first degree felony punishable by imprisonment in the state prison for a term which is a minimum mandatory term of 5, 10, or 15 years and which may be for life.

§76-5-406. Sexual intercourse, sodomy, or sexual abuse without consent of victim - Circumstances.

An act of sexual intercourse, rape, attempted rape, rape of a child, attempted rape of a child, object rape, attempted object rape, object rape of a child, attempted object rape of a child, sodomy, attempted sodomy, sodomy upon a child, attempted sodomy upon a child, forcible sexual abuse, attempted forcible sexual abuse, sexual abuse of a child, attempted sexual abuse of a child, or simple sexual abuse is without consent of the victim under any of the following circumstances:

(1) the victim expresses lack of consent through words or conduct;

(2) the actor overcomes the victim through the actual application of physical force or violence;

(3) the actor is able to overcome the victim through concealment or by the element of surprise;

(4) (a) (i) the actor coerces the victim to submit by threatening to retaliate in the immediate future against the victim or any other person, and the victim perceives at the

time that the actor has the ability to execute
this threat;

(b) as used in this subsection "to retaliate"
includes but is not limited to threats of
physical force, kidnapping, or extortion;

(5) the victim has not consented and the actor
knows the victim is unconscious, unaware
that the act is occurring, or physically unable
to resist;

(6) the actor knows that as a result of mental
disease or defect, the victim is at the time of
the act incapable either of appraising the
nature of the act or of resisting it;

(7) the actor knows that the victim submits or
participates because the victim erroneously
believes that the actor is the victim's spouse;

(8) the actor intentionally impaired the power
of the victim of the victim to appraise or
control his or her conduct by administering
any substance without the victim's
knowledge;

(9) the victim is younger than 14 years of age;

(10) the victim is younger than 18 years of
age and at the time of the offense the actor
was the victim's parent, stepparent, adoptive
parent, or legal guardian; or

(11) the victim is 14 years of age or older, but not older than 17, and the actor is more than three years older than the victim and entices or coerces the victim to submit or participate, under circumstances not amounting to the force or threat required under Subsection (2) or (4).

§76-5-407. Married persons' conduct exempt - "Penetration" or "touching" sufficient constitute offense.

(1) The provisions of this part do not apply to conduct between person married to each other, except for purposes of this part, persons living apart pursuant to a lawful order of a court of competent jurisdiction are not considered to be married.

(2) In any prosecution for unlawful sexual intercourse, rape, rape of child, object rape of a child, or sodomy, any sexual penetration or in the case of sodomy, rape of a child, or object rape of a child any touching, however slight, is sufficient to constitute the relevant element of the offense.

(3) In any prosecution for sodomy on a child, sexual abuse of a child, or aggravated sexual abuse of a child any touching, even if accomplished through clothing, is sufficient to constitute the relevant element of the offense.

APPENDIX B
GLOSSARY

GLOSSARY OF SEX TERMS AND PHRASES

ABNORMAL SEX- generic term covering all criminalized or disvalued sexual behaviors, with the exceptions of adultery and fornication.

ACCOST- term used by police and prosecutors to describe approaches in public, by males or females, for sexual solicitation.

AGE OF CONSENT- statutory age, differing from state to state, which defines the legal capacity of a minor to give informed consent to sexual relations; to have sexual relations, even with consent, with a minor below the age of consent constitutes a crime (see statutory rape.)

ANDROGEN- male sex hormone.

ANDROGYNOUS- possessing both male and female primary and/or secondary sex characteristics.

ASEXUAL- uninterested in sex.

ASEXUALIZATION- castration.

BISEXUAL- one who engages in or is interested in both heterosexual and homosexual behaviors.

CARNAL KNOWLEDGE OF A MINOR- charge brought against an adult who has had copulative or sodomistic relations, no matter how slight the penetration, with a child under the age specified in a given jurisdiction.

CASTRATION- asexualization; surgical excision of the male testes.

CELIBACY- state of sustained virginity; refraining from sexual relations and/or marriage, often for religious reasons.

CHANCROID- visible symptom of venereal infection.

CHASTITY BELT- a device designed to prevent intercourse, at one time locked around a woman's genitals while her husband (father) was away.

CHILD MOLESTER- person, usually male, who seeks sexual satisfaction from very young children.

CLITORIDECTOMY- surgical removal of all or part of clitoris.

COHABIT- formerly used as euphemism for regular or at least repeated copulation between a male and female not married to each other; later tended to be restricted to such couples when living together.

COHABITATION, NONMARITAL- unmarried heterosexual couple domiciling together, usually without affront to community standards.

GLOSSARY

COITUS INTERRUPTUS- withdrawal of the penis from the vagina before emission to prevent unwanted pregnancy.

COMMON-LAW MARRIAGE- relationship legally recognized in some jurisdictions in which certain legal rights inhere to the spouses and, in some cases, children after a statutorily defined period of living together openly, as if a marriage had taken place.

COMMUNITY STANDARDS- phrase used by the U.S. Supreme Court which would define material as pornographic and subject to criminal sanction if patently offensive in a given area.

CONDOM- contraceptive device placed over penis to prevent entry of semen into woman's body; also used for prevention of venereal disease (hence known as prophylactic); rubber (lately, especially promoted to avoid AIDS disease.)

CONJUGAL VISIT- sexual activity between a prison inmate and visiting spouse.

CONSENSUAL ACTS- generic term covering acts between two or more persons that take place by mutual consent, with no threat or use of force, usually restricted to acts between adults.

CONSUMMATE- the process of completing the marital union by having sexual intercourse.

RAPE

CONTINENCE- refraining from sexual relations by act of will

CONTRACEPTIVE- a device, medication, or method of preventing pregnancy.

DEFLORATION- intercourse with a virgin.

DEVIATE, SEXUAL- one whose sexual drive or focus is directed toward socially unaccepted channels, most often used for child molester.

DIAPHRAGM- a contraceptive device inserted into body of woman to prevent fertilization.

DOUBLE STANDARD- value system that was more tolerant of male sexuality or promiscuity than female.

EJACULATION, PREMATURE- emission of seminal fluid either before penetration or before readiness of female partner; ejaculation praecox.

ERECTION- the state of the sexually stimulated, tumescent penis; term is sometimes used when there is stimulation and hardening of clitoris or nipples.

EROGENOUS ZONES- areas of body particularly sensitive to sexual stimulation

GLOSSARY

EROTOGRAPHOMANIA- conduct in which major sexual satisfaction is derived from viewing sexually explicit paintings, sculpture, or other objects.

EROTOLALIA- deriving major sexual satisfaction from talking about or listening to talk about sex.

EROTOMANIA- compulsive interest in sexual matters

EROTOPHILIC- strong interest in and concentration on erotic matters.

EROTOPHOBIC- afraid of sex, hostile to evidences of sexuality.

ESTROGEN- female sex hormone.

EUNUCH- an emasculated male, asexualized, castrated.

EXHIBITIONIST- one deriving sexual satisfaction from the showing of one's genitals to unwilling viewers; dicky waver, flasher.

EXTRACOITAL- sexual connection between male and female not involving penetration of the vagina; may be oral, anal, intermammary, interfemoral, or other.

EXTRAMARITAL- sex outside of marriage by a married person, adultery.

RAPE

FLAGELLATION- a form of sadomasochism in which sexual satisfaction is obtained from whipping or being whipped.

FOREPLAY- stimulation by touching, licking, tickling, pinching, kissing, or in some other form, prior to copulation, and not as an end in itself.

FORNICATION- copulation between a male and a female neither of whom is married.

FRENCH ENVELOPE- contraceptive, particularly a condom.

FRIGIDITY- inability to respond to sexual stimulation.

GERONTOSEXUALITY- abnormal desire of a younger person for sexual relations with a much older male or female.

GONORRHEA- venereal disease characterized by an emission from the penis; clap.

HEBEPHILIA- focusing of the sex drive on very youthful boys or girls; Lolita syndrome.

HEBEPHENIA- mental disease at onset of menarche characterized by uncontrolled sexual promiscuity.

GLOSSARY

HERMAPHRODITISM- possession of some male and some female sex organs by one person; ambiguity as to whether the individual is male or female.

HETEROSEXUAL pertaining to individual sex drive or sex drive oriented toward gratification with other sex.

HOMOSEXUALITY- pertaining to individual or sex drive oriented toward gratification with same sex.

HOOKER- a prostitute

HYMEN- the membrane which closes the opening to the vagina in virgin; cherry.

HYPERSEXUALITY- oversexed; nyphomaniac (female) satyriasis (male)

HYPOPLASIA GENITALIA- very small genitalia; micro-penis.

IMPOTENCE- a condition in which the male is physiologically or psychologically unable to get or maintain an erection at the time of intercourse; occasionally used to describe the female.

INCEST- sexual relations between persons of close blood kinship, relationahip; legally extended to relationships by adoption or through marriage, other than between spouses.

RAPE

INDECENT ASSAULT- any uninvited touching of the genitals, buttocks, or breasts.

INTERCOURSE- term usually restricted to penile-vaginal copulation.

INTRAUTERINE DEVICE- contraceptive which prevents sperm from entering the womb; IUD.

INTROMISSION- the act of introducing semen into the vagina; often used as synonymous with heterosexual copulation.

JOHN- customer of a prostitute, usually used for heterosexual prostitution; trick is sysonym for homosexual and heterosexual customer.

NECROPHILIA- sexual fantasiers about or overt sexual contact with dead bodies.

NOCTURNAL DREAMS- (fantasies, ecstasies)- sexually stimulating dreams, in male usually resulting in ejaculation.

NYMPHOMANIA- compulsive, excessive, deisre for sexual intercourse in female.

ONANISM- masturbation; term has also been used for coitus interruptus.

ONE-NIGHT STAND- term for one-time, nonaffectional, almost mechanical impersonal sex

GLOSSARY

relationship, ususally restricted to homosexual
encounters.

OPEN COHABITATION- unmarried couples living
together without secrecy or circumspection.

ORALISM- oral eroticism.